WITHDRAWAL

NEW DIRECTIONS FOR STUDENT SERVICES

John H. Schuh, *Iowa State University*
EDITOR-IN-CHIEF

Elizabeth J. Whitt, *University of Iowa*
ASSOCIATE EDITOR

Helping African American Men Succeed in College

Michael J. Cuyjet
University of Louisville

EDITOR

Number 80, Winter 1997

JOSSEY-BASS PUBLISHERS
San Francisco

HELPING AFRICAN AMERICAN MEN SUCCEED IN COLLEGE
Michael J. Cuyjet (ed.)
New Directions for Student Services, no. 80
John H. Schuh, Editor-in-Chief
Elizabeth J. Whitt, Associate Editor

ISSN 0164-7970   ISBN 0-7879-9883-4

NEW DIRECTIONS FOR STUDENT SERVICES is part of The Jossey-Bass Higher and Adult Education Series and is published quarterly by Jossey-Bass Inc., Publishers, 350 Sansome Street, San Francisco, California 94104-1342. Periodicals postage paid at San Francisco, California, and at additional mailing offices. Postmaster: Send address changes to New Directions for Student Services, Jossey-Bass Inc., Publishers, 350 Sansome Street, San Francisco, California 94104-1342.

New Directions for Student Services® is indexed in College Student Personnel Abstracts and Contents Pages in Education.

SUBSCRIPTIONS cost $54.00 for individuals and $90.00 for institutions, agencies, and libraries. See Ordering Information page at end of book.

EDITORIAL CORRESPONDENCE should be sent to the Editor-in-Chief, John H. Schuh, N243 Lagomarcino Hall, Iowa State University, Ames, IA, 50011.

Cover photograph by Wernher Krutein/PHOTOVAULT © 1990.

Jossey-Bass Web address: http://www.josseybass.com

Manufactured in the United States of America on Lyons Falls Turin Book. This paper is acid-free and 100 percent totally chlorine-free.

July 3, 2000

CONTENTS

EDITOR'S NOTES

In their 1987 article on counseling black men, Parham and McDavis referred to African American (or black; the terms will be used interchangeably in this volume) men as "an endangered species" (p. 24). The negative social factors they describe give evidence to the important role of higher education in addressing this issue. It is a significant irony that although a number of these negative factors, such as high unemployment and underemployment, can be remedied by successful completion of college, the impact of such other negative factors as poorer primary and secondary educational opportunities and severe financial hardships can cause many black men to fail to gain access to college or, if admitted, to be underprepared for higher education's academic rigor. A focused agenda to assist black men in entering *and completing* college is in the best interests of the students, the institutions, and society at large.

The actual number of African American men enrolled in the nation's colleges and universities has been increasing slightly during the 1990s, but both the percentage (ranging from 3.5 percent to 3.8 percent) and the number (from 485,000 to 550,000 out of fourteen million students; *Chronicle of Higher Education,* 1997) are disturbingly low and small enough to be perceived as fragile. Given that frailty, higher education administrators concerned about this issue are seeking ways to nurture and retain those African American men who are successful in coming to the campus. This volume offers a look at the status of black men in the college environment and provides a number of important suggestions of ways in which higher education administrators and faculty can work together to enhance the probability that more African American men will successfully matriculate.

In Chapter One, I present a brief description of the status of African American men on predominantly white campuses and a review of some of the general concerns contributing to their less-than-desirable status at those institutions. In particular, a comparison between African American men and African American women emphasizes the difference in the relative gains of these two groups. This chapter also examines the responses of more than twenty-four hundred African American men to the survey items on the College Student Experiences Questionnaire (CSEQ) and compares them to similar data reported by African American women and white students.

In Chapter Two, Mary F. Howard-Hamilton presents a series of developmental theories: traditional theories (Chickering, Perry, Kohlberg, and Holland, to name a few), two Africentric theoretical frameworks, Erikson's psychosocial development theory, and Bandura's social learning model. She then describes how each of these theoretical models has served, or failed to serve, African American men. Additionally, she offers a number of suggestions as to how a self-efficacy theory-to-practice approach can successfully contribute to African American men's development on the campus.

In Chapter Three, Janice Dawson-Threat examines a number of factors affecting the classroom academic achievement of African American males. Using a model of racial identity formation, she explores a number of experiences that have proven successful in making the classroom environment more supportive of black men, focusing on three particular topics: application of students' personal experiences, acceptance of differences, and addressing black manhood issues.

In Chapter Four, Bruce D. LaVant, John L. Anderson, and Joseph W. Tiggs describe the benefits of mentoring initiatives and programs for African American men. They then profile a number of successful mentoring programs—some exclusively for black men, some serving black men along with other students—and explain their benefits and applicability to other campuses. The chapter also offers a number of general recommendations regarding mentoring of African American males.

In Chapter Five, E. Michael Sutton and Melvin C. Terrell explore the various opportunities for leadership development on predominantly white college campuses. They examine the relative experiences of African American men in leadership roles in campuswide organizations, in organizations with a focus on minority student issues, and in historically black Greek fraternities. They also present the results of a survey of perceptions on leadership among African American male students at two public, predominantly white universities that demonstrate the relationship between leadership in black fraternities and leadership in campuswide clubs.

In Chapter Six, Sharon Fries-Britt presents an often-overlooked picture of the experiences of gifted African American men, particularly those factors that can positively or negatively affect retention of these special students. She then describes the features of the Meyerhoff Program, one of the premier programs in the country for talented black male students.

In Chapter Seven, Dawn R. Person and Kenya M. LeNoir focus on a particular college population that often includes a disproportionately high number of black men: college athletes. They describe the special challenges and benefits these men encounter because of their status. They also present the results of a study of African American male athletes, examine a number of initiatives that have proven successful in abetting retention of black male athletes, and present three different models for organizing such initiatives.

In Chapter Eight, I present a brief summary of the contents of the other seven chapters in the book, capturing the essential elements of each author's main points and identifying several of the common themes presented throughout this volume. This chapter also offers an annotated listing of several books that may give the reader further insight into some of these themes.

One special word of caution as you begin this book: remember that generalities can be dangerous if they are used to extrapolate from individual examples or a small group to a larger population. While the issues raised in this volume are serious concerns that can apply to significant numbers of black men, these issues do not apply in the same way to *all* black men. The reader who is concerned about the need to attend to African American men on predominantly white campuses need only remember that the characteristics of each of these men consists of three equally important factors: his common human traits shared with all men and women, his black male cultural attributes, and his unique individuality.

Michael J. Cuyjet
Editor

References

Chronicle of Higher Education, Aug. 29, 1997 (in vol. 44, no. 1).
Parham, T. A., and McDavis, R. J. "Black Men, an Endangered Species: Who's Really Pulling the Trigger?" *Journal of Counseling and Development,* 1987, *66* (1), 24–27.

MICHAEL J. CUYJET is an associate professor in the Department of Educational and Counseling Psychology at the University of Louisville. A former student affairs practitioner for more than twenty years, he has served in both campus activities and general student affairs at several universities.

*Efforts to assist minority students on the campus may not address
some particular needs unique to African American men. Examination
of some of their behaviors and attitudes that may differ from those of
other students, particularly African American women, is important.*

African American Men on College Campuses: Their Needs and Their Perceptions

Michael J. Cuyjet

A significant amount of attention is devoted to the circumstances of students of ethnic minority status at predominantly white colleges and universities. As the largest group among these students, African American students have received a considerable amount of that attention. From Willie and McCord's work from a quarter century ago (1972), through Jacqueline Fleming's landmark study in 1984, to the research of a host of more recent writers, the state of black college students has been examined, many of the detrimental obstacles have been exposed, and numerous remedies have been implemented. One concern, however, has been less apparent among this analysis of African American college students: the disparity between the accomplishments of men and women within this population.

The Disproportion of Black Men

A cursory look around most predominantly white campuses (unless one is standing in a location frequented by the football and basketball athletes) probably reveals the fact that black women attend college in proportionally larger numbers than black men. The most recently available figures from the U.S. government and the American Council on Education corroborate such an observation. Among the more than fourteen million students enrolled in American colleges and universities in 1994, black men have the lowest male-to-female proportion when compared to all other ethnic groups. Only 38 percent of black students are male; corresponding percentages for the male segment of other ethnic groups are 49 percent for Asians, 44 percent for Hispanics, 42 percent for Native Americans, and 45 percent for whites (*Chronicle of Higher Education,* 1997). Additionally, in 1994, at each degree level—associate, bachelor's, master's, doctoral, and first-professional—black men, compared to women, also represent a lower proportion of their ethnic population receiving degrees than do Asians, Hispanics, or Native Americans (National Center for Education Statistics, 1996). In a particularly glaring example, among those receiving professional degrees, African American men are the only ethnic group in which men do not outnumber women. This statistic is not an anomaly; in a similar example among the nation's freshman class of 1995 black men have lower numbers compared to their female counterparts than Native Americans, Asians, Hispanics, or whites (*Chronicle of Higher Education,* 1997).

These disparities have a number of significant, far-reaching implications, and the two most significant appear to be in the areas of employment and social status. Mincy (1994) indicates that, compared to that of whites, the college entry rate of black men has fallen since the late 1970s, being 20 percentage points lower than that of white men in 1988. He also suggests that this trend is indicative of growing racial gaps in employment and earnings, gaps that he states generally decrease with greater educational attainment of blacks. Meaningful work is not only important because of the economic results from successful employment; work in the United States is a major measure of achievement. As Hill (1992) writes in his work on the rites of passage of African American men, "A man's worth in America has been based on his ability to provide" (p. 44). Not only is African American men's social status diminished by their lesser ability "to provide" from positions of economic stability, but this status is further negatively affected by the disproportion of men obtaining higher education degrees, resulting in a reduced pool of potential marriage partners for the growing number of African American women who are completing college degrees and moving into occupational positions comparable to such academic levels.

Why black male representation on America's college campuses is so proportionally low is a result of a number of factors, which can be sorted into two basic categories: those preventing black men from ever getting to college in the first place, and those leaving them somewhat underprepared when they arrive on the campus and thus contributing to the higher rate of attrition often experienced by African American men. Among the former group (the proportion of black men that never get a chance to consider attending college), some of the more substantial barriers include a high rate of incarceration, disproportionate high school dropout rates, a high rate of homicide, and serious health problems—such as black men having a higher rate of cancer than any other group in the United States (Parham and McDavis, 1987).

Among those African American men who do make it to college, a significant portion of the group are burdened with what can be generally characterized as an "underpreparedness" for the academic challenges of postsecondary education. This stems from a number of conditions: attending academically poorer elementary and secondary schools, lowered expectations of peers and significant adults toward academic achievement, peer pressure to disdain educational accomplishments and education as an outcome, financial hardships limiting educational access, lack of appropriate role models, and other barriers owing to racism. We can also add to this list what Lee (1991) refers to as developmental disadvantage: those social, cultural, and economic forces that combine to keep black men from attaining traditional masculine roles and that therefore prevent them from mastering crucial developmental tasks in childhood and adolescence that, in turn, negatively affect their social, academic, and career successes later in life.

The Need for Special Care

Whatever the reasons for their relatively low numbers, those black men who do arrive on the campus may need some special nurturing to help them adjust and adapt to the collegiate community. One very critical adjustment is in the campus environment itself: to make that campus environment less hostile than is the prevalent American community to black men in general and those from inner-city backgrounds in particular. As Majors and Billson (1992) state, "social science literature has tended to view black males negatively. Analysis of the social condition of black males in America all too often proceeds from a deficit model" (p. 106). It will be a major step forward if we can get even a small part of the American public to understand that this portrayal is a gross injustice to the majority of the African American men depicted by its images. A worthwhile place to start this reeducation of the American public is among the faculty, staff, and students of our campuses.

Those campus administrators concerned about this issue are presented with a twofold agenda: first, the need to provide a nonthreatening environment for African American men where their higher expectations of success can be nurtured and reinforced; and second, the task of reeducating the majority of the community about the inaccuracy of generally held perceptions about black men. To address the first matter, the campus must become a place that solidly conveys a positive reinforcement to African American men, not the unsupportive, unsympathetic, and unapproachable environment described in some of the research (Fleming, 1984; Wasson, 1990). Campus administrators have a clear obligation to overcome the common message so often conveyed in almost all aspects of American life "convincing inner-city black males that they are merely an 'endangered species,' expected to drop out of school, forbidden to apply to college, destined to be unemployed, and somehow to be excused for not accepting responsibility as men." (Hopkins, 1997, p. 79). Student affairs administrators and their academic administration counterparts should take great care to develop an understanding of African American men's culture and then develop effective interventions based on that new understanding. Such efforts need not always be separate and discrete; they can be the same as those used to assist white male students, they may be adaptations of majority programs with certain accommodations to black male culture, or certain situations may call for unique efforts focused on the specific needs of African American men. Examples of successful programs are detailed in other chapters in this book. In particular, LaVant, Anderson, and Tiggs describe a number of programs in Chapter Four that foster positive mentoring relationships, and Fries-Britt describes one of the country's premier programs for undergraduate African American men in Chapter Six.

To truly address the second part of this agenda—changing the popularly held perception of African American men—an overt campaign must be initiated on predominantly white college campuses to counter the institutionalized, generally negative image of black men accepted by almost every segment of the American population. Hopkins (1997) reminds us that "black male culture is almost always interpreted to mean dire trouble and social unrest, and seemingly most Americans are comfortable with this perception" (p. 78). One of the first things we may need to address in making the college experience less marginalizing for African American men is to recognize the broad acceptance and institutionalization of these negative perceptions of black men as threatening, unfriendly, and less intelligent than any other distinguishable segment of the American population. Ironically, one of the more critical populations requiring assistance in changing attitudes about the merits and abilities of African American men is that of African American men themselves. Kunjufu (1986) documents the "failure syndrome" by which as early as the fourth grade black males become aware that schools do not invest in their learning process. Many of these young men internalize these attitudes and develop an inferior perception of their own abilities and aspirations as compared to others. This is analogous to what Shelby Steele (1991) calls the "anti-self," which he describes as "an internal antagonist and saboteur that embraces the world's negative view of us, that believes our wounds are justified by our own unworthiness, and that entrenches itself as a lifelong voice of doubt" (p. 41). As Tyrone Taborn observes (quoted in Green and Wright, 1991), "From inner-city school kids to the freshmen at Harvard University, an overwhelming percentage of black students simply do not believe they are as smart as whites" (p. 29). Success in this effort could make the college environment the first community in which some African American men encounter a positive perception of themselves and their culture.

Male and Female Differences

As mentioned in the beginning of this chapter, one of the ways to address the issues related to the adjustment of African American men on the campus is to focus on the discernible differences between African American men and African American women. One example is how American men and women in general often differ in the process of their personal development. The work of such researchers as Gilligan (1982); Chordorow (1974); and Belenky, Clinchy, Goldberger, and Tarule (1986) demonstrates some fundamental differences in how men and women socialize, make moral decisions, and process information. This difference may be exacerbated among African Americans by sociological factors that inhibit the development of African American men. In an examination of the adolescent development of black males, Lee indicates how racism and socioeconomic disadvantage can contribute to a "complex set of interacting historical and social factors that often inhibit success" in completing those tasks normally associated with personal development (1994, p. 35). According to Havighurst (cited in Lee, 1994), these tasks include achieving a masculine or feminine social role, desiring and achieving socially responsible behavior, acquiring a set of values and an ethical system as a guide to behavior, and preparing for an economic career. The result of encumbered ability to achieve personal developmental tasks is that African American men's roles, behaviors, values, and economic outlooks are often unlike those of their white male counterparts and can even be quite dissimilar to those of African American women. Lee adds that successful completion of normal developmental tasks can be further hampered by negative school experiences such as "ineffective teaching strategies and educators' predetermined negative views of black males and their learning potential" (p. 36). Although Lee's research focuses primarily on these problems in the secondary schools, the impact of a similarly negative educational environment in postsecondary education can be equally harmful.

Thus, the developmental differences that may be generally expected between men and women are made even greater by factors affecting black men. These differences appear even more drastic as black men adopt alternative behaviors to compensate for the "normal" behaviors denied them because of racism, socioeconomic disadvantage, or a combination of the two. Majors and Billson (1992) refer to "subjective cultural realities for black males" (p. 109), especially those including violence, and call for researchers to study them further, particularly in the context of how masculinity is defined. In contributing to this understanding of black masculinity, Hopkins (1997) calls particular attention to the roles of power (or powerlessness) and resistance in black male culture. On a more positive note, Jeff (1994) suggests that the development of African American male youth can best be understood in the context of Africentrism, particularly through certain ethical principles he has labeled the "seven Rs": respect, responsibility, reciprocity, restraint, religion, rhythm, and redemption (p. 103).

Reviewing Black Men's Survey Responses

One practical way of further examining the needs of African American men in the college community, particularly as their needs may differ from those of African American women, is to examine the differences in how they express themselves in their assessment of the campus environment. There are numerous studies of African American men on college and university campuses. Usually, these studies select particular variables to examine, such as retention, educational attainment, attitudes and values, or psychosocial changes

(Pascarella and Terenzini, 1991). However, for the purpose here of simply representing how African American men perceive the campus environment as an introduction to the specific topics represented in the subsequent chapters of this volume, it is unnecessary and probably inappropriate to delve into the interpretations of these researchers on various aspects of the lives of black male college students and their female and white peers. A better perspective may be found in raw data from a large-scale survey of the actual perceptions of these students about the campus and its various components. Such a picture of the campus is presented by the data of the College Student Experiences Questionnaire (CSEQ); hence, the balance of this chapter examines some of the information gleaned from the data compiled through comprehensive administration of this survey instrument.

The CSEQ is a 191-item instrument for gathering self-reported information from students about their background, aspirations, and status in college. It also asks about the activities in which they engage, the facilities they use, the opportunities they find for learning and development, and the quality of their relationships among various groups on campus. Students are also asked to estimate the extent of progress they have made in general education, intellectual skill development, personal and social development, knowledge of science and technology, and vocational preparation (Kuh, Vesper, Connolly, and Pace, 1997). Since the first edition in 1979, more than 350,000 students have completed the CSEQ instrument. The third edition of the instrument was introduced in 1990. The current edition of *Revised Norms for the Third Edition* (Kuh, Vesper, Connolly, and Pace, 1997) is based on the responses of 50,188 students from sixty-six colleges and universities who completed the CSEQ between 1990 and 1996. The data are reported in six categories, the first five of which are based on the Carnegie Classification Index (Carnegie Foundation for the Advancement of Teaching, 1994) to include research universities (RUs), doctoral universities (DUs), comprehensive colleges and universities (CCUs), selective liberal arts colleges (SLAs), and general liberal arts colleges (GLAs). A sixth category is labeled "urban universities" (URBs) and represents institutions "located in metropolitan settings and having as their primary mission addressing the educational, economic, and social needs of people within commuting distance" (Kuh, Vesper, Connolly, and Pace, 1997, p. 9). Among the students represented in the revised norms, 6 percent (2,851) identify themselves as black or African American. The percentage of black students ranges from 1.9 percent of the students at selective liberal arts colleges to 8.4 percent at general liberal arts colleges and 10.8 percent at urban universities.

The Center for Postsecondary Research and Planning at Indiana University, the repository of these data, provided this author with a report on a sample of all the test respondents in the 1990–1996 period who identified themselves as African American. This sample of 6,765 students consists of 2,431 men (35.9 percent) and 4,308 (63.7 percent) women, with 26 subjects (0.4 percent) who did not indicate gender. Although statistical analysis of this sample against the data used to generate the revised norms was not available for this purpose, visual review of the two sets of data reveals a number of areas in which the differences between African American men and African American women and between African American students and their non–African American peers seem apparent, even though the general student data were broken down by institution type and the data on black students were for the entire sample. Of particular interest are items that reveal differences in areas where student affairs practitioners can offer some reasonable remedies that may be particularly appealing to African American men.

Course Learning and Experience in Writing. Three of the items in the section of the survey on course learning indicate that African American men do not perform as well as African American women in these academic endeavors. Whereas 61.4 percent of African American women very often "Took detailed notes in class," only 43.9 percent of African American men indicated that they do so. Conversely, twice the percentage of men as women (1.5 percent to 0.7 percent) indicate they never took detailed notes in class. Similar to the above item, more than twice the percentage (4.7 percent to 2.3 percent) of African American men compared to their female peers say they never "Underlined major points in the readings," while half again as many (44.7 percent to 27.6 percent) women as men say they do so very often. This may indicate that African American men come to the institution without the same basic study habits that other students have, placing them at a distinct disadvantage regardless of their cognitive abilities. Black men may also fall behind in the "social" aspect of the learning process if they fail to develop linkages with other students. This seems to be indicated by the responses for the item "Tried to explain the material to another student or friend," in which 65.8 percent of African American women say that they do so often or very often, yet only 57.0 percent of African American men do.

Three items from the experience-in-writing section of the survey also support the notion that African American women perform some academic activities better than African American men. Although 33.8 percent of African American women declare they "Spent at least five hours or more writing a paper (not counting time spent in reading or at the library)," only 23.0 percent of African American men do so very often. In a similar activity, 26.4 percent of black women very often "Revised a paper or composition two or more times before you were satisfied with it" but only 16.7 percent of black men do. If the inference is that African American men need help in persevering with some of their composition assignments, this might be an area where a campus can make a particular effort to provide easy access to assistance in developing such skills. However, one other item may show that black men are not as likely as black women to take the initiative in finding help with their writing. On the item "Asked other people to read something you wrote to see if it was clear to them," only 21.4 percent of African American men say they do this very often, compared to 32.5 percent of African American women.

Student Union. If student affairs practitioners are seeking a way to make contact with black male students in particular, one item in this group is revealing. It appears that African American men frequent the student union for recreational purposes considerably more than African American women do. Almost twice the percentage of black men (36.1 percent to 19.3 percent) indicate that they "Played games that were available in the student union or center (ping-pong, cards, pool, pinball, etc.)" very often or often compared to black women. Fifty-two percent of African American women never play such games, while only 30 percent of men never do.

Athletic and Recreation Facilities. By far, the survey category with the greatest difference between African American men's and African American women's responses is in the use of athletic and recreational facilities. Of the ten items in this group, black men indicate much greater participation in all areas surveyed. The difference in percentages was the lowest for "often" and "very often" (54.3 percent to 40.6 percent) responses to the item "Was a spectator at college athletic event," which is not a participatory activity.

On the item "Set goals for your performance in some skill," 60.5 percent of African American men say they do so often or very often, compared to 35.7 percent of African American women. More than twice as many African American men as African American women (49.8 percent to 23.4 percent) say they often or very often "Followed a regular schedule of exercise, or practice in some sport, on campus." Almost three times as many (38.7 percent to 13.3 percent) black men as black women often or very often "Used outdoor recreational spaces for casual and informal *individual* athletic activities." A similarly disproportionate percentage of black men (37.0 percent to 10.1 percent) often or very often "Used outdoor recreational spaces for casual and informal *group* athletic activities." Twice as many African American men (50.6 percent to 24.3 percent) often or very often "Used facilities in the gym for individual activities (exercise, swimming, etc.)" as their female counterparts. Similarly, these men "Used facilities in the gym for playing sports that require more than one person" often or very often two and one-half times (51.9 percent to 20.4 percent) as much as women. African American men often or very often "Sought instruction to improve your performance in some athletic activity" at a higher rate (34.2 percent to 6.9 percent) and also often or very often "Played on an intramural team" at a rate more than four times (34.2 percent to 6.9 percent) that of black women. Black men often or very often "Kept a chart or record of your progress in some skill or athletic activity" at three times the rate (21.8 percent to 6.7 percent) of black women.

It is important to note that not only did black men indicate much higher participation in these athletic and recreational activities than did black women, but on four of these items one-half of all African American men surveyed said they participate often or very often. It would seem that providing adequate, available athletic and recreational facilities, both outdoor and indoor, may be a key factor in making the college environment a welcoming one for African American men.

Clubs and Organizations. Although African American men demonstrate a much more active interest in athletic and recreational activities than African American women, the responses to items regarding other extracurricular activities reveals a reverse trend, with the ratios by which women are more active not nearly as drastic. Nonetheless, on four items black women seem to be more willing to partake in campuswide activities. Nearly one-half (47.5 percent) of black women often or very often "Looked in the student newspaper for notices about campus events and student organizations" while only 39.7 percent of black men say they do so. Similarly, a somewhat larger percentage (44.4 percent to 36.7 percent) of African American women than African American men often or very often "Attended a program or event put on by a student group." Only 30.4 percent of black men say they often or very often "Read or asked about a club, organization, or student government group," but 39.6 percent of black women do. Black women often or very often "Attended a meeting of a club, organization, or student government group" to a greater degree (38.3 percent to 31.1 percent) than do black men. Black women often or very often "Worked on a committee" in greater numbers than black men (24.3 percent to 18.2 percent). It is thus possible to infer that these are not significant areas for any special efforts aimed at supporting black men specifically. The items do leave room for speculation as to the degree to which these activities pertain to campuswide clubs or groups in contrast to organizations that are focused on the campus's Africa American community. In Chapter Five, Sutton and Terrell explore the relationship between black men's leadership participation in "minority" organizations, particularly in fraternities, and their participation in campuswide groups.

Personal Experiences. Three items from this section of the survey illustrate differences in how African American men and African American women relate to their peers in regard to personal issues. Even though a majority of both groups indicated that they often or very often "Told a friend why you reacted to another person the way you did," the divergence of 69.4 percent women and 55.3 percent men demonstrates a considerable difference in this behavior. Similarly, while 56.5 percent of African American women often or very often "Sought out a friend to help you with a personal problem," only 39.6 percent of African American men do so. And 24.3 percent of black men often or very often have "Been in a group where each person, including yourself, talked about his/her personal problems," yet 36.0 percent of black women do this often or very often. As was observed earlier in this chapter, these distinctions may be a result of the differences in how men and women are socialized in American society. On the other hand, it would be prudent to see if attempting to provide an atmosphere where African American men can develop relationships in which personal interactions are more prevalent may make the campus climate less marginalizing to them.

Demographics. Among the demographic information requested in this instrument, black men seem to have dissimilar response patterns on three items. In reply to the question, "At this college, up to now, what have most of your grades been?" only 16.5 percent of African American men indicate "A, A−, or B+" while 24.0 percent of African American women give this response. The range of responses at the various institutions in the norms is from 35.3 percent at urban institutions to 52.0 percent at selective liberal arts colleges.

Conversely, the 18.9 percent of African American men who indicate that their grades are "C, C−, or lower" is one and one-half times the percentage indicated by African American women (12.5 percent) and well above the range (2.7 percent to 11.7 percent) of the responses in the norms. This information may point to one of the more critical needs of African American men on campus: assistance in their academic work.

These last two items do not demonstrate major differences between African American men and African American women; however, as revealing demographic information about black men, it seems prudent to consider their ramifications on black male college success. On the item "Did either of your parents graduate from college?" only 17.5 percent of African American men indicate that *both* parents are graduates, compared to a range of 21.0 percent to 50.1 percent in the norms. Thus, it may be that parental college graduate role models are less prevalent for black men than for their white counterparts; and if role modeling is important to academic success, it is possible that this discrepancy has a considerable affect on African American men.

It is also possible that financial concerns could distract African American men from their grades. When asked "About how much of your college expenses this year are provided by your parents or family?" the norms for those who have "all or nearly all" of those expense paid by someone else ranges from a low of 29.3 percent to a high of 41.9 percent, while only 23.3 percent of black men responded with that answer. The 44.4 percent of black men who have "none or very little" of their college expenses paid by others is considerably higher than the percentage for any norm group except urban school students. Relieving the distraction of securing adequate college financial support may be a very important element in the efforts of student affairs practitioners focusing on the particular needs of African American men.

Summary

Although their actual numbers have been increasing through the 1990s (*Chronicle of Higher Education,* 1997), African American men represent a disproportionately small percentage of the total college population and a much smaller male versus female percentage than in any other ethnic group. This underrepresentation in higher education has significant impact on black men, particularly in employment opportunities and earning ability. It also negatively affects their social status in American society and especially in their relations with African American women, who are achieving somewhat greater success through educational attainment. Among those African American men who are successful in getting to the college campus, many arrive in a state of unpreparedness resulting from poorer schooling; financial hardships; and other social, cultural, and economic disadvantages.

To provide assistance to this cadre of African American men, college and university administrators should concern themselves both with providing a nonthreatening environment for black men on the campus and with engaging in a serious effort for the entire campus community, including black men themselves, to dispel the common stereotypes. Because black men and black women are different in some important ways, these efforts to assist black men on the campus may have to include some special elements that apply to the needs of men alone.

One way to assess the needs of African American men on campus is to review what a sample of these young men have said about their experiences at colleges and universities across the country. The data collected using the College Student Experiences Questionnaire provides such information from thousands of such students. A cursory examination of these data reveals that African American men differ from African American women in a variety of areas on the campus.

Student affairs administrators need to study this group of students carefully and resist inclinations to treat African American men and African American women the same way. Some attention to the special areas of interest of black men may yield surprising results in overcoming the far-too-common marginalization of these students.

References

Belenky, M. F., Clinchy, B. M., Goldberger, N. R., and Tarule, J. M. *Women's Ways of Knowing: The Development of Self, Voice, and Mind.* New York: Basic Books, 1986.

Carnegie Foundation for the Advancement of Teaching. *A Classification of Institutions of Higher Education.* Princeton, N.J.: Carnegie Foundation for the Advancement of Teaching, 1994.

Chordorow, N. "Family Structure and Feminine Personality." In M. Z. Rosaldo and L. Lamphere (eds.), *Woman, Culture, and Society.* Stanford, Calif.: Stanford University Press, 1974.

Chronicle of Higher Education, Aug. 29, 1997 (in vol. 44, no. 1).

Fleming, J. *Blacks in College: A Comparative Study of Students' Success in Black and in White Institutions.* San Francisco: Jossey-Bass, 1984.

Gilligan, C. *In a Different Voice: Psychological Theory and Women's Development.* Cambridge, Mass.: Harvard University Press, 1982.

Green, R. L., and Wright, D. L. "African American Males: A Demographic Study and Analysis." Paper presented at the W. K. Kellogg Foundation National Workshop on African-American Men and Boys, Mar. 27, 1991.

Hill, Jr., P. *Coming of Age: African American Male Rites-of-Passage.* Chicago: African American Images, 1992.

Hopkins, R. *Educating Black Males: Critical Lessons in Schooling, Community, and Power.* Albany: State University of New York Press, 1997.

Jeff, Jr., M.F.X. "Afrocentrism and African-American Male Youths." In R. B. Mincy (ed.), *Nurturing Young Black Males: Challenges to Agencies, Programs, and Social Policy.* Washington, D.C.: Urban Institute Press, 1994.

Kuh, G. D., Vesper, N., Connolly, M. R., and Pace, C. R. *College Student Experiences Questionnaire: Revised Norms for the Third Edition.* Bloomington: Center for Postsecondary Research and Planning, Indiana University, 1997.

Kunjufu, J. *Countering the Conspiracy to Destroy Black Boys.* Chicago: African American Images, 1986.

Lee, C. C. *Empowering Young Black Males.* Ann Arbor, Mich.: ERIC/CAPS, 1991. (ED 346 184)

Lee, C. C. "Adolescent Development." In R. B. Mincy (ed.), *Nurturing Young Black Males: Challenges to Agencies, Programs, and Social Policy.* Washington, D.C.: Urban Institute Press, 1994.

Majors, R., and Billson, J. M. *Cool Pose: The Dilemma of Black Manhood in America.* San Francisco: New Lexington Press, 1992.

Mincy. R. B. (ed.). *Nurturing Young Black Males: Challenges to Agencies, Programs, and Social Policy.* Washington, D.C.: Urban Institute Press, 1994.

National Center for Education Statistics. *Digest of Education Statistics.* Washington, D.C.: U.S. Department of Education, National Center for Education Statistics, 1996.

Parham, T. A., and McDavis, R. J. "Black Men, an Endangered Species: Who's Really Pulling the Trigger?" *Journal of Counseling and Development,* 1987, 66 (1), 24–27.

Pascarella, E. T., and Terenzini, P. T. *How College Affects Students: Findings and Insights from Twenty Years of Research.* San Francisco: Jossey-Bass, 1991.

Steele, S. *The Content of Our Character: a New Vision of Race in America.* New York: Harper-Collins, 1991.

Wasson, R. "Implications from a Black Student Culture for More Effective College Teaching: Black Voices in the White Institution." Paper presented at the annual meeting of the American Anthropological Association, New Orleans, Nov. 29, 1990. (ED 337 090)

Willie, C. V., and McCord, A. (eds.). *Black Students at White Colleges.* New York: Praeger, 1972.

MICHAEL J. CUYJET *is an associate professor in the Department of Educational and Counseling Psychology at the University of Louisville. A former student affairs practitioner for more than twenty years, he has served in both campus activities and general student affairs at several universities.*

itioners and graduate teaching faculty need appropriate theories
correlate to the developmental issues affecting African American
nts and that can be translated into practice as programs to
enhance the matriculation rate of these students.

Theory to Practice: Applying Developmental Theories Relevant to African American Men

Mary F. Howard-Hamilton

African American men have been vanishing from our communities, elementary and secondary schools, and college campuses the past two decades in alarming numbers. Many of these boys and young men leave school before completing their high school diplomas, thus thrusting them into a vicious circle of oppression, depression, and despair. Although the variables surrounding the disappearance of African American men have been identified, relatively few student affairs administrators, counselors, and graduate preparation faculty have identified specific theories as well as programming or intervention goals, objectives, and techniques to ameliorate the problems these students encounter once they reach the college campus. It is typically assumed that because an African American man has been admitted to the institution, he has overcome the odds and has the ability to successfully matriculate and graduate. However, what is not known by most administrators and counselors is that he may be internalizing tremendous personal burdens similar to those of the noncollege-bound group of African American men.

The issue of loss is one usually associated with African American men. It is quite probable that these men have witnessed a homicide in their own community or social circle, and that they know African American men who are incarcerated and others who are on drugs. Obviously, these societal dilemmas decimate the ranks of the African American male. The men who survive may still harbor emotional scars from fighting institutional racism and seeing their African American brothers fall victim to the system. Therefore, it is incumbent that the student affairs administrator, counselor, and graduate preparation program faculty learn and teach the theories that connect with appropriate practices to empower African American men on campus. Many of these men are struggling with their search for identity (Cross, 1991, 1995; Howard-Hamilton and Behar-Horenstein, 1995; Erikson, 1980), attempting to develop resistance strategies for personal and academic survival (Robinson and Howard-Hamilton, 1994), and attempting to find persistence in activities that are foreign to them but in which mastery could make them self-efficacious (Bandura, 1977).

Based upon these complex psychosocial issues that African American men are grappling with, some traditional student development theories may not be applicable for this group. Furthermore, operable theories of student development still need to be created for African Americans; "when traditional theories are used in working with black students, conclusions are often reached that are not accurate" (McEwen, Roper, Bryant, and Langa, 1990, p. 434). Additionally, the same authors state, "as student affairs professionals attempt to make theories of human and student development more inclusive of other populations, it seems more important to create theories rather than to modify or revise existing ones" (p. 435). That is the purpose of this chapter: to present established theories that are inclusive of the needs of African American men. Additionally, two Africentric models are detailed, and suggestions for interventions and activities are provided that can be used to create a supportive and comfortable campus climate for these men as well.

Conventional Developmental Theories

Traditional student development theories have been the guiding paradigms for our profession for more than forty years. Institutions have embraced and adopted theories developed by Chickering, Perry, Kohlberg, Holland, Super, Loevinger, and Sanford, to name a few. Most of these theories do not reflect the sociocultural perspectives and realities of a multicultural society (Cheatham and Berg-Cross, 1992). For example, when we use the career development theories of Super and Holland, is there a connection made for students of color who have not had the privilege of observing successful persons in business, creative arts, or education such that they can have a clear point of view or perspective when it comes to their career choice? It is often assumed that most students can make a career choice because they have had the appropriate vocational mentoring. When we apply the moral reasoning concepts of Kohlberg to college-age students, how often do we consider the moral dilemma process for students of color? For example, if an African American man who is debating whether or not to challenge a rule for the sake of a friend or loved one then decides not to challenge the "status quo," is she or he not at a higher level of moral development? It could and should be noted that many African American students do not challenge the system and established rules because this process would put the student in serious jeopardy with the law thanks to socioeconomic subjective bias. In other words, decisions made by whites to break the law may not lead to severe penalties; however, if an African American man breaks the same law there is a considerable amount of subjective bias in how the system interacts with the black man. Typically, the penalties for the person of color are more severe. Therefore, when applying Kohlberg's moral reasoning principles, the person's race, cultural background, and socioeconomic status should be taken into consideration before assuming that lower stages of development are in effect: "African American student development is arguably distinct from student development in general and hence development of this cohort is not adequately accommodated in existing theories and models of student development" (Cheatham and Berg-Cross, 1992, p. 173).

Given the increasing numbers of students of color on our college campuses, it may be dangerous in applying existing theories (which are based upon the traditional values and philosophies of a western worldview and researched with predominantly white participants) to students of color (Harris, 1995; McEwen, Roper, Bryant, and Langa, 1990). Incorporating the developmental issues of African American students into existing paradigms can be attained, but according to McEwen, Roper, Bryant, and Langa nine dimensions need careful scrutiny and attention before this process begins:

1. *Developing ethnic and racial identity:* inculcating ethnic identity and information and facts on African self-consciousness development
2. *Interacting with the dominant culture:* discussing acculturation, assimilation, and association with white students on campus
3. *Developing cultural aesthetics and awareness:* understanding and appreciating other cultures as well as one's own
4. *Developing identity:* enhancing one's own unique and diverse characteristics, societal interaction, and group identification
5. *Developing interdependence:* establishing personal relationships amid some separation from immediate family but with development of extended campus family
6. *Fulfilling affiliation needs:* satisfying African American students' social needs outside the campus community
7. *Surviving intellectually:* challenging African American students to compete with those who had educational privileges preparing them for the academic rigors of college
8. *Developing spirituality:* understanding the role and importance of religion and spirituality in the growth and development of African Americans
9. *Developing social responsibility:* coming face-to-face with real and perceived social inequities, thus becoming social advocates on campus (1990, p. 430)

These nine dimensions provide evidence that perspectives on ethnicity and ethnic influences on student growth and development should include differences in consciousness, self-worth, and philosophy of life (Jones, 1990). When teaching student development theory or integrating a theoretical framework into student affairs division activities, it is important to include these nine dimensions so that students of color feel included and so that majority students can learn about multiculturalism and have their ethnocentric perspectives challenged. If, for example, you are using Chickering or Erikson as significant developmental models, you would integrate dimensions four and five above into the traditional paradigms by encouraging interaction with a peer group that enhances racial and ethnic pride. This group connection should lead to an enhanced sense of racial pride and sensitivity to other cultures. As contacts and connections with those students who embrace a high level of identity pride are established, it is important to have the student of color gain further understanding of other diverse groups. This exploration may lead the student to disconnect with the traditional lessons taught by family members and to branch out and explore other perspectives as well as nurture new friendships. This may be difficult for a student of color because of the very close family network. Therefore, the traditional theories need to be flexible and expand for the continued identity-development process that the students of color may encounter throughout their undergraduate years due to societal, cultural and traditional, and developmental challenges within their racial or ethnic group.

African American men have suffered immeasurably in our society. As noted in Chapter One, they are not being afforded the full benefit of education and societal promotion, they have the lowest life expectancy and it is declining, homicide is the leading cause of death, and the fact of endemic incarceration leaves few role models in the community (Lee, 1996; Parham and McDavis, 1987). In addressing these issues, the most salient concerns affecting African American men are (1) education, (2) career concerns, (3) health and safety, and (4) self-esteem or personal growth and development.

Africentric Theoretical Frameworks

There are four developmental models that could be useful when designing interventions to enhance the development of African American men on college campuses in these areas:

1. Cross's Nigrescence Theory (1991, 1995)
2. Robinson and Howard-Hamilton's Africentric Resistance Model (1994)
3. Erikson's Identity Development Model (1980)
4. Bandura's Social Learning Model (1977)

Each theory is described below with an appropriate application to practice.

The Nigrescence Theory. The Nigrescence paradigm is a resocializing process in which there is "the transformation of a preexisting identity (a non-Africentric identity) into one that is Africentric" (Cross, 1995, p. 97). The word *Nigrescence* is derived from the French for a sense of negritude, or the state of being black.

There are five stages in the Cross model of Nigrescence. The first is *pre-encounter,* in which there is an antiblack attitude and endorsement of the Eurocentric cultural perspective. The person in this stage may be very self-centered and individualistic and may determine progress by how far one moves through the system, rather than how the system treats the group. Stage two is *encounter,* in which there is a significant emotional life-changing situation or circumstance that is likely to be a motivating factor in challenging previous antiblack cultural beliefs and that consequently prompts a change in personality. *Immersion-emersion* is the third stage, in which there is a commitment to personal change and to demolition of the old Eurocentric cultural frame of reference, developing as well as embracing a new and healthier Africentric cultural perspective. In the fourth stage, *internalization,* issues presented in the previous stages are challenged successfully and a healthy Africentric identity is embraced. The internalized identity helps "(a) to defend and protect a person from psychological insults that stem from having to live in a racist society, (b) to provide a sense of belonging and social anchorage, and (c) to provide a foundation or point of departure for carrying out transactions with people, cultures, and human situations beyond the world of Blackness" (Cross, 1995, p. 113). The fifth stage is *internalization-commitment,* which gives the individuals an opportunity "to translate their personal sense of Blackness into a plan of action or general sense of commitment" (Cross, 1995, p. 121).

Practical applications of the Nigrescence model can be implemented stage by stage once there has been a behavioral assessment of the level of development the African American man displays. In the preencounter stage, the learning environment should be highly structured and supportive, with a mentor who avoids confrontation and moralizing in processing the person's behaviors or the experiential activities. The mentor and student should also avoid any premature discussion of significant racial, ethnic, or cultural differences. Culture-specific programming activities may challenge and support this individual, for example, African American History Month speakers focusing on cultural groups and social behaviors, and self-evaluation of one's own cultural background. At the encounter stage, the African American man can act as an instructor by providing information on what is "good" about one's culture, accompanied by "good" things about other cultures and engagement in cross-cultural activities and programs. It is also important at this stage to challenge any misconceptions about other racial ethnic groups by enhancing cross-cultural communication. The immersion-emersion stage should be cognitively challenging and encourage autonomous self-review for the African American man. Since the person may be experiencing a pro-black, antiwhite perspective, the activities the mentor engages in should explore the impact of this one-sided way of thinking. To help the person successfully emerge from this narrow frame of reference, it is important that the African American man be exposed to culturally sensitive individuals from other races to serve as resource persons and to work in small groups with other men to share their feelings of resentment and anger so they may find a point in which openness, sharing, understanding, and acceptance occurs. The final two stages should include continuous opportunities for discussion with persons from other cultural groups, helping the men find a supportive network of persons who have similar beliefs, and to promote social change by helping others moving through the phases of Nigrescence and becoming positive role models within the African American and white communities.

The Africentric Resistance Model. The second Africentric theoretical framework that can be used to develop programs for African American men is the Africentric model, constructed by Robinson and Howard-Hamilton (1994). The Africentric resistance paradigm is based upon Robinson and Ward's Resistance Modality Model (1991) and the Nguzo Saba value system developed by Maulana Karenga (1980). According to Karenga, the Nguzo Saba represents a basic value system that is African in origin and enables individuals to establish direction and meaning in their lives. The seven basic values that constitute the Nguzo Saba system (Table 2.1) are *Umoja* (unity), *Kujichagulia* (self-determination), *Ujima* (collective work and responsibility), *Ujaama* (cooperative economics), *Nia* (purpose), *Kuumba* (creativity), and *Imani* (faith).

Robinson and Ward (1991) designed the resistance modality model, which is used in combination with the Africentric paradigm to promote personal growth. The resistance modality model is based upon the philosophy that there are healthy forms of psychological and personal resistance to negative and deleterious caricatures of one's race or culture that can promote personal growth and modify one's perception of the self and one's sense of community. A strong sense of Africentric identity involves connection with and knowledge of one's cultural, racial, and historical roots. Where there are positive images of oneself and one's culture, there is a healthy resistance developed to refute messages that attempt to demean, destroy, or detract from that culture. In this case, the person is self-governed and self-determined to maintain a healthy mental perspective and not let others rule one's destiny.

Environments contribute to overwhelming feelings of powerlessness within the person, and this sense of powerlessness often impacts the entire community in an unhealthy form of resistance, which may be exhibited as violence, anger, or complete despair and depression: "In this case, self-determination is not a primary factor because the person's self-image is largely shaped and defined by external and economic forces that have their roots in racist ideology" (Robinson and Howard-Hamilton, 1994, p. 328).

According to Nobles (1980), an Africentric view represents a self-affirmation, reawakening, and rebirth of personal beliefs and behaviors. Essentially, one can be pro-African and not antiwhite. Africentricity represents a strong connection to one's spirituality and kinship via African culture; it culminates in a shared belief that "I am because we are, therefore, I am." The self and others are seen as interconnected. Thus, an interdependent rather than independent cultural perspective is endorsed in a spirit of collective responsibility and generosity.

The Africentric paradigm could be the framework for providing programs that lead to successful matriculation of African American men on our college

Table 2.1. Africentric Resistance Modality Model

Survival/Oppression	Liberation/Empowerment
Isolation and disconnectedness from the larger African American community	Unity with African people that transcends age, socioeconomic status, geographic origin, and sexual orientation (Umoja)
Self-defined by others (the media, educational system) in a manner that oppresses and devalues blackness	Self-determination through confrontation and repudiation of oppressive attempts to demean self; new models used to make active decisions that empower and affirm self and racial identity (Kujichagulia)
Excessive individualism and autonomy; responsibility; the self is seen in connection with the larger body of African people, sharing a common destiny (Ujima)	Collective work and racelessness
"I got mine, you get yours" attitude	Cooperative economics advocating a sharing of resources through the convergence of the "I" and the "we" (Ujaama)
Meaninglessness in life; immediate gratification to escape life's harsh realities, the use of "quick fixes"	Purpose in life that benefits the self and the collective, endorses delaying gratification as a tool in resistance (Nia)
Maintaining status quo; replicating existing models, although they may be irrelevant	Creativity through building new paradigms for the community, through dialogue with other resisters (Kuumba)
Emphasis on the here and now, not looking back and not looking forward, myopic vision	Faith through an intergenerational perspective where knowledge of the history of Africa and other resisters and care for future generations gives meaning to struggle and continued resistance (Imani)

Source: Robinson and Howard-Hamilton (1994), p. 329. Copyright © 1994 American Counseling Association. Reprinted with permission. No further reproduction authorized without written permission of the ACA.

campuses. This model would interweave elements of the theoretical Nguzo Saba value systems with certain aspects of resistance that can initiate and promote psychological health and satisfying interpersonal relationships for African American men within and between cultures. The Nguzo Saba principles and value system could be the guiding mission, goals, and objectives for these men throughout their college career and beyond.

Various programs can be developed to enhance the Africentric identity development among African American men: (1) a big brother (upperclassman) and little brother (freshman) support system, which could allow boys in elementary and middle schools to have a young adult role model (*Ujima, Imani, and Ujaama*); (2) an Africentric reading group (*Kujichagulia, Nia,* and *Kuumba*); (3) group counseling (*Ujima*); (4) African American community service (*Umoja*); (5) an African American men's retreat (*Umoja*); (6) an African American men's residence hall floor (all seven principles); (7) a weekend for fathers or male family members and students (all seven principles); and (8) an African American male faculty and student workshop (*Umoja,* in addition to other principles depending upon the purpose and goals of the workshop).

These are just a few of the activities that can be designed to support and challenge the African American male student as well as move him through the various stages of Nigrescence and the Africentric model. Other programs should be developed to encourage group harmony, communication, and support. Also connected to the Africentric model is enhancing one's knowledge of the African heritage. This can be accomplished by reading cultural literature and discussion groups. A limited list of readings are noted at the end of the chapter, and there are many other biographies, films, and self-help materials that can be added to the list. Eventually, the men should begin reading literature from other cultures so they can gain a greater understanding of other traditions and customs. It should also be noted that too much emphasis on African American philosophy, history, literature, and culture may be detrimental. Through his study on African American men, Johnson (1993) uncovers that there is a reverse relationship with grades and African self-consciousness. The higher the Africentric self-consciousness orientation, the less likely the student is to achieve academic success. These men, who internalized the strong Africentric identity, rejected the Eurocentric education system because it was incongruent with their attitudes and values. It is imperative that there be a strong group leader who can model Africentric behaviors and coexistence with persons from other cultures, and who can promote the philosophy that knowledge is power.

Psychosocial Development Theoretical Frameworks

We turn next to existing developmental theories and transform them to fit the needs of African American men.

The Identity Development Model. The epigenetic principle (Erikson, 1980) is a psychological, biological, environmental, and age-related ground plan in which growth occurs when serious choices and difficult challenges are encountered. The issues or crises that arise are bipolar competing alternatives. In other words, there is an emotional decision-making process at each stage as the ground plan unfolds (Erikson, 1980). Each crisis arises at a special time during one's life until all crises have been adequately resolved and the individual forms a functioning healthy personality.

Erikson posits eight stages that people encounter from birth to adolescence or young adulthood. Stage one is basic trust versus mistrust. There is trustfulness as far as others are concerned and trustworthiness as far as oneself is concerned. Successful resolution of this stage leads to a sense of hope as to whether or not society is basically trustworthy. The second stage is autonomy versus shame and doubt, in which the person must move beyond self-consciousness and inferiority toward independence and pride. The resolution at this stage is desire, determination, and pleasure in life. The third stage is initiative versus guilt, in which the question is "What kind of person am I going to be?" There are a number of role models that the person observes and emulates to find the personality and behaviors that are a good fit. The resolution of this bipolar crisis is purpose or determination (initiative) with a goal in life. The fourth stage, industry versus inferiority, involves mastery of certain tasks that take skill, patience, and cooperation with others. The outcome of this stage is a sense of competence in which the person has developed "the pleasure of work completion, steady attention, and persevering diligence" (Erikson, 1980, p. 91). The fifth stage is identity development versus identity diffusion; although identity development is a lifelong task, establishing a workable framework is predominant during adolescence and young adulthood, extending into the traditional college years (Widick, Parker, and Knefelkamp, 1978). It is at this stage the individual asks "Who am I" and "What will I be?" The term *identity crisis* has been used to describe the cognitive confusion and personal dissonance the person encounters at this stage. Erikson also describes this behavior as "motivating uncertainty" because the individual is trying to make ideological and career decisions to organize the personal world. The resolution of this stage evolves into fidelity, or constancy, and allegiance to a particular set of beliefs and comfort with who one is and who one wants to become. The sixth stage, intimacy versus isolation, is frequently intertwined or synchronous with self-definition. Erikson says that "the condition of a true twoness is that one must first become oneself" (1980, p. 101). The resolution of this stage leads to sensitivity to nurturing personal relationships. The critical components that mediate resolving one's identity are (1) activities and programs that support the individual in decisions regarding interests, abilities, and personal beliefs; and (2) experiences that pave the way for making commitments (Widick, Parker, and Knefelkamp, 1978). Erikson's two remaining stages of the eight occur typically from age thirty-five to retirement: generativity versus self-absorption, and integrity versus despair.

It is the early stages of Erikson's model that should be revisited and explored when working with African American men. Specifically, the stages of trust versus mistrust (during childhood) and identity versus identity diffusion (during adolescence). Courtland Lee (1996) states that "black males are often prevented from mastering both these crucial universal and race-specific developmental tasks in childhood and adolescence. In turn, this lack of mastery retards their academic, career, and social success in the later stages of life" (p. 17). During the childhood phase, Lee notes several tasks and issues that should be adhered to when working with African American men:

(1) recognition of self and others based on color; (2) incorporate racial labels into evolving self-concept; (3) recognize, identify, and label social inconsistencies

e.g. racism, discrimination, prejudice; (4) recognize and develop of skills for negotiating multi-racial environments and bicultural experiences, each containing mixed and contradictory messages; (5) forge an appropriate and healthy identity in the face of racism, discrimination, prejudice; and (6) fine-tune sensing and judging skills to screen out or transform negative racial/color images and messages. [During adolescence, when the identity-formation process is taking place, the added steps to development are to] refine healthy identity which transforms and/or transcends societal messages of inferiority, pathology, and deviance based on color, race and/or culture) [and to] strengthen skills for negotiating bicultural and multicultural environments. [Lee, 1996, p. 17]

The Social Learning Model. It is evident that most African American men have not had the opportunity to engage in activities that elevate their level of self-esteem, self-worth, and self-efficacy. Bandura reports that "expectations of personal self-efficacy determine whether coping behavior will be initiated, how much effort will be expended, and how long it will be sustained in the face of obstacles and aversive experiences" (1977, p. 191). If these men are nonetheless diligent in activities that they view as intimidating, they may gain understanding that the system has psychologically instilled a debilitating belief (namely, that only a select few can aspire to certain levels of prominence), and they may find themselves actually enhancing their own belief that they can achieve against the odds.

It is important to understand that one can assume that certain outcomes result from given behaviors; this is known as "outcome expectancy" (Bandura, 1977). An "efficacy expectation" is confidence that a behavior can be successfully employed to generate outcomes. These definitions are separated because individuals can believe that a certain task gives rise to specific results, but if they have serious reservations regarding the ability to tackle the specific activity then their behavior is not influenced or changed. Bandura says that "the strength of people's convictions in their own effectiveness is likely to affect whether they will even try to cope with given situations" (1977, p. 193). If individuals are provided with appropriate skills and incentives, they increase their ability to choose stressful situations and find coping mechanisms. Strengthened efficacy outcomes and expectations are derived from four primary sources of information: (1) performance accomplishments, (2) vicarious experience, (3) verbal persuasion, and (4) emotional arousal (Figure 2.1).

Performance accomplishment is successful personal completion of a set of activities or experiences. Once individuals successfully complete a task, they may seek other challenges. Furthermore, failures are limited or reduced because although they may encounter a crisis, their motivation is strengthened and "even the most difficult obstacles can be mastered by sustained effort" (Bandura, 1977, p. 195).

Another way individuals learn how to master difficult situations is by observing a live role model engaging in a "high risk" situation without a neg-

Figure 2.1. Efficacy Expectations: Major Sources of Efficacy Information and the Principal Sources Through Which Different Modes of Treatment Operate

Source of Information	Mode of Induction

Performance accomplishments
- Participant modeling
- Performance desensitization
- Performance exposure
- Self-instructed performance

Vicarious experience
- Live modeling
- Symbolic modeling

Verbal persuasion
- Suggestion
- Exhortation
- Self-instruction
- Interpretive treatments

Emotional arousal
- Attribution
- Relaxation, biofeedback
- Symbolic desensitization
- Symbolic exposure

Source: Bandura (1977), p. 195. Copyright © 1977 by the American Psychological Association. Adapted with permission.

ative outcome. Individuals can then role-play and put themselves in the shoes of the role model completing the task (Bandura, 1977). This method is called vicarious experience; persons observing vicariously believe that if other individuals can complete the task, they should be able to accomplish the activity as well. What is also very important to note regarding this activity is that if people from significantly diverse backgrounds or characteristics can succeed, then those who observe have a sound reason for heightening their own sense of self-efficacy.

The power of verbal persuasion or suggestion to sway or control human behavior is easily and readily used in our society (Bandura, 1977). However, this method of self-empowerment is not as effective as those emerging from one's own attainments because the actual experience was not completed by the individual listening to the persuader. However, verbal persuasion (interaction) coupled with corrective actual performance (independent action) by the person with low self-esteem can engender a sense of self-efficacy.

Fear, anger, resentment, and hostility are evoked if people are placed in oppressive situations. Stressful and exhausting activities generally evoke emotional arousal; depending on the controlling factors, valuable information can be presented pertaining to personal competency. If individuals are placed in debilitating situations and are emotionally aroused adversely, their performance is also negatively affected. The psychological state of the persons in an environment that they view as nonsupportive negatively impacts their behavior and demeanor: "Behavioral control not only allows one to manage the aversive aspects of an environment. It also affects how the environment is likely to be perceived" (Bandura, 1977, p. 199). If individuals perceive their environment as less threatening, then their fearful emotions are reduced during potentially stressful events and increased coping capabilities are recognized and enhanced.

The social learning model has direct application to African American men because it is the importance of having role models and learning experiences relevant to men's lives that empowers this group. A mentor program can be established for the men so they are exposed to a career person who could make a significant impact on their future vocational choices (Howard-Hamilton, 1993). Additionally, mentors could provide a challenging stimulus to get the men to engage in difficult situations with support to process and discuss the outcomes of the activity. This balance and support is a form of verbal persuasion, primarily positive self-talk within a group or one-on-one. Another method of creatively engaging the men is to have them keep a journal of their feelings, concerns, anxieties, and successful endeavors (Howard-Hamilton, 1993). The mentor can be the support person, by listening to some of the reflections noted by the younger man. Reviewing the journal regularly helps the man tap into and elicit emotional arousal and learn how to cope with anger, frustration, excitement, and satisfaction. (See Chapter Four for more on mentoring relationships.)

Johnson (1993) says that the SAT verbal score is a better indicator of academic success for African American men than the math score. Concomitantly, African Americans may be influenced by the oral or verbal tradition of storytelling and sharing of family history that is characteristic of the African worldview and perspective. This skill can be heightened and honed by implementing the verbal persuasion and vicarious experience methods of the social learning model using bibliotherapy and video therapy. Observing tapes of Martin Luther King Jr. and Malcolm X and hearing their speeches and reading books on African Americans (preferably men) who have overcome major life obstacles and battles not only improves listening and reading skills but also provides modeling even if there are few African American role models living in the community. Upper-class African American men on campus who are involved with campus activities or a fraternity may be possible mentors for incoming students. In a recent study, Taylor and Howard-Hamilton (1995) note that African American men who participate in Greek letter organizations embrace a stronger sense of Africentric self-consciousness and racial identity compared to those not in Greek letter organizations. The members of these organizations should be trained as peer counselors for other African American men so that they can have a supportive network of academically successful upperclassmen. This activity also bridges a gap between Greeks and non-Greeks on the college campus. (See Chapter Five for more on the influences of African American men's Greek letter organizations.)

Summary

When researchers began their studies on the decimation of the African American male population, numerous strategies for survival and success were provided. At a minimum, programs and activities should be created to assist African American men in becoming more tolerant in interracial group settings (Farrell, 1996); disseminate information on career and work options in underrepresented areas such as math, science, and engineering (Stein, 1996); match them with African American male role models (Harris, 1996; Johnson, 1993; Morgan, 1996); and provide them with an opportunity to work with other African American men in defining who they are, where they fit in the campus environment, and how they can find balance and harmony with themselves and others.

A theory-to-practice approach in which the models are adapted for racial, ethnic, gender, and cultural fit could be the missing link to providing group interventions for African American men. These restructured or new theories should enhance chances for academic success and degree attainment for these men.

Using the self-efficacy approach, African American men benefit from mentors (to model appropriate behaviors), role-playing real-life scenarios, and opportunities to engage in challenging situations with supportive individuals so that they can succeed. In conjunction with heightening their level of confidence, the men learn more about their racial ethnic heritage and how to resist negative messages about African American men by engaging in the resistance modality and Nigrescence models. The overall goals are for the men to have a healthy identity and be able to persevere against the odds society has placed in their paths. Identity resolution is the culmination process for a strong positive belief in who one is and what one will become. If the African American man has all of the appropriate developmental tools to use when faced with life's challenging situations, he should be able to rise above drugs, incarceration, homicide, gang violence, and racism by finding strength from within and from others who care and have persevered against the odds.

References

Bandura, A. "Self-Efficacy: Toward a Unifying Theory of Behavioral Change." *Psychological Review,* 1977, *84,* 191–215.

Cheatham, H. E., and Berg-Cross, L. "College Student Development: African Americans Reconsidered." In L. C. Whitaker and R. E. Slimak (eds.), *College Student Development.* New York: Haworth, 1992.

Cross, W. E. *Shades of Black.* Philadelphia: Temple University Press, 1991.

Cross, W. E. "The Psychology of Nigrescence: Revising the Cross Model." In J. G. Ponterotto, J. M. Casas, L. A. Suzuki, and C. M. Alexander (eds.), *Handbook of Multicultural Counseling.* Thousand Oaks, Calif.: Sage, 1995.

Erikson, E. *Identity and the Life Cycle.* New York: Norton, 1980.

Farrell, C. "Is Racism a Male Thing? Study Suggests That Men Have Less Tolerance Than Women." *Black Issues in Higher Education,* 1996, *13* (16), 22–24.

Harris, S. M. "Psychosocial Development and Black Male Masculinity: Implications for Counseling Economically Disadvantaged African American Male Adolescents." *Journal of Counseling and Development,* 1995, *73,* 279–287.

Harris, W. G. "African American Males in Higher Education: Reframing the Issue." *Black Issues in Higher Education,* 1996, *13* (16), 92.

Howard-Hamilton, M. F. "African American Female Athletes: Implications and Imperatives for Educators." *NASPA Journal,* 1993, *30,* 153–159.

Howard-Hamilton, M. F., and Behar-Horenstein, L. "Counseling the African American Male Adolescent." *Elementary School Guidance and Counseling Journal,* 1995, *29,* 198–205.

Johnson, R. E. "Factors in the Academic Success of African American College Males." Unpublished doctoral dissertation, College of Education, University of South Carolina, 1993.

Jones, W. T. "Perspectives on Ethnicity." In L. V. Moore (ed.), *Evolving Theoretical Perspectives on Students.* San Francisco: Jossey-Bass, 1990.

Karenga, M. *Kawaida Theory.* Los Angeles: Kawaida Publications, 1980.

Lee, C. C. *Saving the Native Son: Empowerment Strategies for Young Black Males.* Greensboro, N.C.: ERIC/Cass, 1996.

McEwen, M. L., Roper, L. D., Bryant, D. R., and Langa, M. J. "Incorporating the Development of African American Students into Psychosocial Theories of Student Development." *Journal of College Student Development,* 1990, *31,* 429–436.

Morgan, J. "Reaching Out to Young Black Men." *Black Issues in Higher Education,* 1996, *13* (16), 16–19.

Nobles, W. "Extended Self: Rethinking the So-Called Negro Self-Concept." In R. Jones (ed.), *Black Psychology.* (2nd ed.). New York: HarperCollins, 1980.

Parham, T. A., and McDavis, R. J. "Black Men, an Endangered Species: Who's Really Pulling the Trigger?" *Journal of Counseling and Development,* 1987, *66,* 24–27.

Robinson, T. L., and Howard-Hamilton, M. F. "An Africentric Paradigm: Foundations for a Healthy Self-Image and Healthy Interpersonal Relationships." *Journal of Mental Health Counseling,* 1994, *16,* 327–339.

Robinson, T., and Ward, J. "A Belief Far Greater Than Anyone's Disbelief: Cultivating Resistance Among African American Adolescents." *Women and Therapy,* 1991, *11,* 87–103.

Stein, S. "What the Census Says About the Black Male." *Black Issues in Higher Education,* 1996, *13* (16), 26–27.

Taylor, C., and Howard-Hamilton, M. F. "Student Involvement and Racial Identity Attitudes Among African American Males." *Journal of College Student Development,* 1995, *36,* 330–335.

Widick, C., Parker, C. A., and Knefelkamp, L. "Erik Erikson and Psychosocial Development." In L. Knefelkamp, C. Widick, and C. A. Parker (eds.), *Applying New Developmental Findings.* San Francisco: Jossey-Bass, 1978.

MARY F. HOWARD-HAMILTON *is an associate professor in the Department of Counselor Education-Student Development Services Program at the University of Florida, Gainesville, Florida.*

Enhancing in-class academic experiences requires understanding the salient nature of race as part of identity formation for African American men and requires the development of good teaching strategies.

Enhancing In-Class Academic Experiences for African American Men

Janice Dawson-Threat

This chapter presents an example of how faculty and others engaged in teaching-learning situations can incorporate student development theory into the practice of teaching. Examples of how one can use a theory to develop in-class activities to enhance learning for African American male students are provided. Application of student development theories to the practice of teaching is not only a method for addressing the cognitive intellectual needs of students but also, as Creamer suggests, an "assist in enhancing their growth and development as individuals encountering life transitions" (1990, p. 10) and should be done intentionally and developmentally. Creamer also informs us that student development theory and the research that supports it can help us "recognize that student behavior is not just a matter of chance and random effect; rather, many aspects of student behavior are observable, measurable, explainable, generalizable, and therefore, to some extent, predictable" (p. 12). Incorporating these theories into classroom experiences creates opportunities for students to explore life's transitions and to cognitively process their own growth and development. Understanding the theory-to-practice process enables teachers to construct a variety of pathways for success for this unique student group.

African American Men and Academic Achievement

Examination of research findings reveals that academic achievement related to African American men in college can be affected by the college's racial environment and whether they are attending a white or black college. Some researchers assert that the student-faculty relationship is important; others indicate that racial identity status is salient and affects students in their

ial development. Some researchers have found gender differences
ales and females in the area of achievement. The remainder of this
presents some of the details of those findings.

Davis (1994) discusses the nature of success for African American men in
terms of environment and academic achievement (citing a study done by Nettles in 1988). The subsample Davis used in his analyses consisted of all the
African American men surveyed in the original study, including 742 black men
who attended both historically black (55 percent) and predominantly white
(45 percent) institutions.

Davis addresses two major questions: (1) How do black men who attend
historically black colleges differ from those who attend predominantly white
ones? (2) Are there differences in the predictors of academic success for these
two groups? His conclusions are that academic achievement can be affected
differently by college racial environment and other college environmental variables. Secondly, the determinants of academic achievement vary between black
men attending black and white colleges. He reports on a study done by Fleming in 1984, which found that African American men benefit socially and academically by attending historically black colleges, whereas attendance at
predominantly white institutions appears to retard the development of African
American men.

Davis (1994) perceives that academic integration (the indicator of students' integration into and satisfaction with their academic environment) is at
the core of understanding the variations in the academic experience and outcomes of black men in higher education. After looking toward a broader inter-
pretation of black students' college experience, Davis found other researchers
who suggested that the student-faculty relationship is what is important for
the success of African American men at both types of institutions. It is critical
that faculty know and understand that some students perceive the environment as nonsupportive and hostile (Allen and Haniff, 1991; Fleming, 1984)
and therefore do not initiate informal contact, particularly outside the classroom setting, and hence do not reap the benefits of the positive effect this kind
of contact can have upon academic performance. Additionally, he informs us
that it is not the amount of time that the student spends with the faculty member but the type of interaction that significantly affects the student's academic
performance. Pollard (1993) notes the work of Chester, done in 1983, that
found "at the college level, African American women had lower aspirations and
reported lower self-esteem than African American men" (p. 347), therefore
indicating that interaction for African American women with faculty and the
college environment is a different experience than for men.

Davis cites other studies whose findings assert that African American students find their racial minority status as salient and feel a sense of alienation
on white campuses. He does not differentiate between men and women on this
point. However, Plummer (1995) reports "a significant difference between
African American male and female adolescents in their expression of preencounter racial identity attitudes, with women endorsing them less than their

male counterparts" (p. 177). Thus, we might interpret from these results that men understand the sociopolitical implications of race in America sooner than women do. However, in a study of forty-one highly successful African American men and women Edwards and Polite (1992) conclude that having a positive and strong sense of blackness and a sense of who they are contributed greatly to their overcoming obstacles, prejudices, and inequities.

It should be noted that black professors may not be any more knowledgeable about psychosocial needs or identity development processes beyond their own personal experience than are white professors, and the ability to use the information in an intentional developmental manner may be outside the range of skills of the majority of professors. Increasing one's knowledge about the formation of identity for African American students, particularly as it relates to men, can be facilitated by either contacting a student development theorist on campus who can assist in learning more about the psychosocial needs of these students or by acquiring related texts and then working with a campus psychologist to learn how to interpret and apply the information. As professors and teachers work directly with African American male students, they must begin enhancing the students' individual successes in the classroom setting.

Understanding Racial Identity Formation

For African American adolescents, racial identity development is a part of the identity formation process (Plummer, 1995). It is believed by some researchers that they do not assume ownership of their racial identity until late adolescence or early adulthood, which for traditional-age students would represent the undergraduate years in higher education. Since the perception of racial status is a salient characteristic, using racial identity theories is appropriate for developing in-class activities to enhance African American student learning, particularly for the men. Since it has been established that there are gender differences in adolescents for physical, intellectual, social, personality, and moral development (Craig, 1992), it stands to reason that there are differences between African American men and women in resolving their racial identity development as well.

Cross's model of Nigrescence, which is the process of developing a black racial identity, functions similarly to Marcia's identity model in that it recognizes "achieved racial identity as a result of a racial identity crisis that involves searching and exploration, and ends in resolution and commitment to an African American identity" (Plummer, 1995, p. 170). However, outside social forces, such as going to college, often require African American adolescents to establish a position on their connection with their race (Plummer, 1995). Professors might be of assistance in helping black male adolescents through this process by helping them make connections between the reality of their lives and the learning experiences that are provided in the classroom setting. Through reflection and comparative analysis with the content of the subject, students can safely search and explore their experiences and then possibly reach some resolution and commitment to an identity. Students can make a conscious decision on their commitment to an African American identity while simultaneously shaping themselves as scholars, intellectuals, and budding professionals.

Theory to Practice in a Classroom Setting

Strange and King (1990) have provided a model, consisting of four steps for moving from theory to practice, that enables a student development professional to function in an intentionally developmental manner. This process can be used in a classroom setting by an individual instructor with a diverse group of students and is flexible enough to be used across disciplines.

The first step in the process is to identify the theories related to the developmental needs of the students enrolled. It is fundamentally important to know theories related on the one hand to teaching and learning styles and on the other hand to the particular subject being taught. Thus the content of the course provided would be theory-driven and would use teaching strategies and assignments that are related to researched and tested methods of learning and simultaneously connected to the life transition experiences students are having while engaged in the scholarly pursuit of knowledge.

When a class contains African American male students, for example, knowing Cross's theory of racial identity development can assist in enhancing their in-class experiences. Several models of racial identity development have been designed or developed to improve upon earlier models (Cross, 1971; Thomas, 1971; Jackson, 1975, Taylor, 1976; Rotheram and Phinney, 1987; Smith, 1989; Parham, 1989a, 1989b; Helms, 1990; Cross, Parham, and Helms, 1991; Parham and Williams, 1993). Knowing other theories related to gender, cognitive development, and person-environment issues is also beneficial and relevant for other represented groups.

Cross's model of black racial identity development (1971, 1978; Cross, Parham, and Helms, 1991) proposes five stages for the black identity development process (see Chapter Two for more explanation). A professor can begin to apply the theory as early as the first-session introductions. Informal assessment enables the professor to tailor instruction to fit learning styles and growth and development needs, and to identify more fully the context and depth from which the student is communicating. Thus, the initial communication can provide some initial insight into the student's racial identity. What follows are examples of classroom activities to facilitate growth at the five stages of the Cross model. Quotes from African American male students in the author's classes offer additional insights.

Preencounter. Students at this stage may reveal that they were raised in a predominantly white setting, or that they are comfortable being the only student (or family) of color in a particular setting. The student may be unable to assign any value or meaning to blackness because its existence outside of the family has not been assigned any significance or value. Being color-blind is easy when color has not been assigned any value. The student may not have received any supportive instruction about the sociopolitical implications of race and may sincerely believe that certain people are in disadvantaged circumstances because they chose them.

During the initial in-class introductions, students are afforded the opportunity to share information about their previous academic experiences. Since most syllabi and classroom strategies have been determined before registration is completed, the second step (using researched information) can allow for flexibility and adjustment of those strategies to meet the reality of the learning styles of the individuals enrolled. This continues the process of going from theory to practice.

Based on substantial research on learning styles and developmental behavioral outcomes, appropriate assignments and strategies for meaningful discussion groups can be developed. Beginning the course with foundational information has the effect of leveling the playing field and affords everyone a common language and reference point for future in-class interaction. Foundational information includes introducing and explaining theories related to the subject or field, defining terms that are particular to the subject, and explaining the processes and procedures commonly used in this field. Students who are in the preencounter mode need far more explanation and opportunity for discovery of sociopolitical and U.S. race relation information in order to communicate beyond the level of opinion in class. Frequent and lengthy class discussions often silence these students as they become aware of their own lack of knowledge. Short research tasks and small group discussions enable them to acquire the information they need in order to gain experience in using their cognitive skill sets, and to acquire confidence in exercising their communication skills. Thus an intellectual environment is created that can provide a safer level of interaction and sharing of new ideas. As one African American male undergraduate said: "Through all the personal experiences that were shared in class, I also learned that some ideas I had coming into the class were not all true or applied to every given situation. The ideas of power and influence are ones which I will always keep in mind."

Encounter. For some students, the consciousness-raising encounters began in their home communities as distinctions emerged between them and their childhood friends who happened to be white. For other students, the encounters began as they changed to the precollege track or school, or their families moved into neighborhoods or communities that were predominantly white. For still others, the same experience is encountered when moving into an all-black setting for the first time. Finally, for some the encounters came on arrival at a mostly white institution in a predominantly white community, or at a mainly black campus coming from a largely white community.

Students who are in the encounter mode benefit greatly from journaling projects, one-minute paper assignments, reflective writing assignments, and interview activities. This process allows them to shift and sort their feelings along with the subject matter of the course, establishing their relationship with the subject or discipline being studied. As another African American male undergraduate says, "I have used my journal writing as a learning experience by writing from a personal standpoint. I've incorporated in my journal articles personal life experiences and thoughts that did not stack well with me throughout my life. The journal articles also lead me to find out more about myself and my feelings. . . . My journal entries were an extension of my personal thoughts and experiences, and it felt very comfortable sharing my thoughts with the class and in the journal."

Immersion. Students at this stage often exhibit heightened levels of intellectualism and a strong desire for developing cognitive understanding, which is often expressed through interest in doing research from a black perspective on a given topic, tracing the Africentric beginnings of a subject. Students in immersion may reveal a breadth of knowledge regarding current black thought on an issue.

Students who are in the immersion mode appreciate the opportunity to enlighten and inform other students with their new learning through in-class discussions, oral reports, presentations, book reviews and reports, research papers, and video and media presentations. In an African American male graduate student's words: "Finally, I am still curious as to why the history text does not cover the struggle of African Americans to acquire higher education as well as the many contributions that African Americans have made to higher education. Well, I guess that's where my job starts as an African American scholar."

Internalization. Students at this stage may question reading lists and units of study that do not include African American and other ethnic perspectives. They may also preface their statements with a descriptor to indicate that the particular thought they are about to share is representative of a larger African American or ethnic perspective and more than their own opinion.

Students who are in the internalization mode need assignments that allow them to do different or additional reading from an African American, or "global," perspective. These students need the opportunity to engage the lecturer in addressing those perspectives, so as to learn that the instructor may have a perspective different from their own: "I had always been aware of, and spoken out about, damaging issues in the black community, but for some images I did not have the proper context or historical background to elaborate at any depth," said one African American male undergraduate student. "This unit provided me with some ammunition for my fight. As a hip hop artist, my industry gets accused of misogyny, misrepresenting the black community, encouraging violence, and destroying the 'moral fiber' of black (they really mean white) youth. This is not entirely correct."

Step three of the process involves the practice of teaching, and interaction between the student's values and those of the professor. Throughout the delivery of the course, students should be provided an environment to explore their values and the values introduced by the course content. They are then able to accept, reject, or revise their understanding. Says an African American male undergraduate: "I learned a lot in this class. I am not, as you have guessed, a person who takes being wrong well. Yet, the way the material explained why I was wrong allowed me to formulate new beliefs. These are beliefs brought about by an increased awareness of the black female struggle. They are, without question, better beliefs than the ones I began with."

Our ability as professors, instructors, and teachers to assist students in their learning and through their life transitions is revealed in step four of the theory-to-practice model, the process of evaluation. Postassessments, summary papers, student-faculty conferences, and teaching-evaluation instruments are ways to obtain information on the effectiveness of the assignments and strategies used in class and their impact upon students' learning and lives. An African American male undergraduate student puts it this way: "This class has brought the awareness to me and placed it in reality. . . . I feel this class has deepened my cause and goals in life, which is to educate and uplift the African American nation."

Enhancing In-Class Experiences for African American Male Students

It is in the interchange between the professor's values and the student's values that the greatest potential for establishing a successful in-class experience for learning occurs. Three components that this researcher recommends for inclusion in every class for African American male students, which can serve as a conduit for facilitating identity development and thus providing positive results and success, are (1) including a safe space for expression of personal experience, (2) facilitating and promoting the understanding of difference, and (3) providing the opportunity to explore black manhood issues.

Personal Experience. It is important for all students to have the experience of expressing this aspect of themselves in the classroom setting. It enables African American men to explore intellectually and academically those issues of preencounter and encounter situations that they have experienced prior to college or during their settling-in process at predominantly white institutions. Attending a largely white institution places the student in an environment that is ripe for encounter experiences because it provides countless opportunities for experiencing racial boundaries (Plummer, 1995).

The students' points of view contributed in class often revolve around friendships with white students in the residence hall, encounters with police and store security personnel, deaths of neighborhood friends, and being able to "fit in" back home when they complete their education. These are a few of the issues that African American men are processing along with their academic subjects. Including this component in a variety of assignments serves as a freeing mechanism for African American male students and aids them in discovering their own voice; it helps establish them as active intellectuals in the class. An African American male undergraduate says: "I found the topic on black men a little more interesting because it was related to my own [interest]. Through the research I did and the thought that I put into my paper, I received new ideas and new learning. I was exposed to so many concepts that I never really considered before. . . . The journal writing served as a learning tool because it gave me a chance to express myself. I was forced to think and formulate ideas."

Difference. Gaining an understanding of difference and being comfortable with it (Dawson-Threat, 1995) is the second component for successful in-class experiences. African American men of college age are keenly aware when others are uncomfortable with their presence in certain settings. Just as white students are not comfortable discussing race in mixed groups (Tatum, 1992), African American men are equally unwilling to become the object of discussion and exploration. African American male college students are concerned about the negative stereotyping that overshadows their genuine identity as intelligent, young black men on the rise.

Even within a college campus setting, the subject of difference for African American men becomes most uncomfortable when discussion pertains to relationships with African American women, "black on black crime," interracial dating, and social hierarchies of race and gender. African American men need to be provided with a comfortable and safe classroom atmosphere to discuss difference as it relates to their home communities and relationships. Their ability to intellectually engage in communication with others that does not result in a negative outcome can assist them in learning to accept difference as a positive descriptor and thus aid them in moving into the immersion stage of Cross's theory. For those already in that stage, these activities can aid in moving out of immersion (though this change is not as outwardly apparent as movement into immersion). "The topic of black women, and the talk about affirmative action were of most concern to me. The struggle to acquire an education for black women affects me as a black man. I feel I have a responsibility to help in any way that I can to overcome oppression of black people trying to get a formal education" (African American male undergraduate student).

Black Manhood Issues. The last and most complicated component for designing enhanced in-class assignments and experiences is to incorporate the issue of black manhood, which relates to constructs of leadership and vocational identity and African American men's ability to determine their place in society. Students express concern about assimilation and separation from their home communities and their abilities to be leaders of men and institutions, and they question whether the leadership skills they are learning enable them to be leaders of other black men. Since African American men perceive their racial identity development as a salient part of their development, they must process new learning and information received in the classroom and connect it to these constructs. The status of their relationship to the information has to be weighed against their own perceived status as black men in society. As an African American male graduate student said, "Recently, I was in a meeting with professionals from another institution and I discussed Cross's theory. At that point, the meeting became an exercise [of] these professionals identifying students on their campus and discussing what stage they were in. It was absolutely astounding to see these white administrators making sense of black students' behavior. It was affirming to witness what appeared to be genuine interest in the theory and how it could relate to assisting African American students."

Assisting students in synthesizing this information and giving them an opportunity to clarify for themselves their future position in society aids in moving them toward internalization. With that achieved, the student feels comfortable with himself and with the processing and filtering of new information and learning received from the class; he has a sense of growth and development (both cognitive and psychosocial) and should appear to be stimulated, focused, and encouraged about his next academic experience.

Plummer (1995) tells us that young adults have reduced reliance upon middle-aged members of groups (such as parents) for influence upon their pattern of development. However, teachers and significant other role models (particularly faculty and student affairs professionals, even if they are middle-aged) become even more important in contributing to students' identity development (Plummer, 1995). According to an African American male undergraduate: "This class was the best class that I have ever taken in my five years here. I learned so much in so little time. My only regret is that I could not take more of your classes. This class has broadened my chain of thought. Don't change a thing! The only recommendation that I have is for you to recruit more *black males* to your classes. It would make a difference in their lives."

Collaboration Between Faculty and Student Affairs Professionals

The final step in the theory-to-practice model is the evaluation or intervention step. One suggestion for completing this phase of the model is to increase the collaborative relationships between faculty and student affairs professionals. Student affairs professionals with expertise in student development theory can serve as consultants for faculty in designing in-class experiences such as role playing, discussion exercises, and simulated town-hall experiences that can incorporate and provide components of developmental theory concurrently with the required content knowledge of the course.

They can also assist faculty in learning about student development theory and how to recognize various stages of development through analysis of themes and reflective writings of students. Additionally, student affairs services can provide group support, cultural programming, and role modeling through employing staff who can assist African American men in transitioning through the college life experience.

Faculty can collaborate with student affairs professionals to enhance faculty members' awareness of development issues for African American men by volunteering to serve on student affairs committees, becoming a speaker and frequent visitor at residence hall programs, and participating in mentoring and retention activities that increase opportunities for informal gatherings between faculty and students. Additionally, faculty can provide assistance in increasing academic integration for African American male students by including them in departmental student organizations and other out-of-class learning opportunities. When necessary, referrals to the student affairs staff for additional support and role modeling should be facilitated for African American male students as soon as a faculty member becomes aware that a student is experiencing difficulty in achieving academic integration.

Summary

By incorporating student development theories into in-class experiences for African American men, faculty can enhance the pathways for success by addressing students' cognitive intellectual needs and by facilitating their growth and development as individuals proceeding through life transitions.

Institutional type does affect student achievement, but student faculty relationships have been shown to contribute a positive effect no matter what the environmental conditions. As faculty learn about environmental variables that affect African American male students, they can contribute to positive outcomes by designing in-class experiences that include racial identity development activities for those students.

Effective interventions include using a theory-to-practice model and incorporating Cross's theory of racial identity development; appropriate teaching strategies; and the three recommended components of including a safe space for the expression of personal experience, facilitating and promoting the understanding of difference, and providing the opportunity to explore black manhood issues. This last component embraces constructs of leadership and vocational identity and increases the opportunity for positive student-faculty interaction and relationships, thereby improving the chances for greater academic integration into department and discipline-based activities. Finally, student affairs professionals and faculty need to collaborate to establish bridges for increasing their understanding of the student affairs services and academic offerings that African American men experience while attending college.

References

Allen, W. R., and Haniff, N. A. "Race, Gender, and Academic Performance in U.S. Higher Education." In W. R. Allen, E. Epps, and N. Z. Haniff (eds.), *College in Black and White*, 95–110. Albany: State University of New York Press, 1991.

Craig, G. *Human Development*. (6th ed). Englewood Cliffs, N.J.: Prentice Hall, 1992.

Creamer, D. G. *College Student Development*. Alexandria, Va.: American College Personnel Association, 1990.

Cross, W. E. "The Negro-to-Black Conversion Experience: Toward a Psychology of Black Liberation." *Black World*, 1971, *20*, 13–27.

Cross, W. E. "The Cross and Thomas Models of Psychological Nigrescence." *Journal of Black Psychology*, 1978, *5*, 13–19.

Cross, W. E., Parham, T. A., and Helms, J. E. "The Stages of Black Identity Development: Nigrescence Models." In R. E. Jones (ed.), *Black Psychology*. (3rd ed.). New York: Harper-Collins, 1991.

Davis, J. E. "College in Black and White: Campus Environment and Academic Achievement of African American Males." *Journal of Negro Education,* 1994, *63* (4), 620–633.

Dawson-Threat, J. "Critical Pedagogy: Teaching 'Difference' in Race and Gender Studies." *Thresholds in Education,* 1995, *22* (3–4), 16–22.

Edwards, A., and Polite, C. K. *Children of the Dream: The Psychology of Black Success.* New York: Doubleday, 1992.

Fleming, J. *Blacks in College: A Comparative Study of Students' Success in Black and White Institutions.* San Francisco: Jossey-Bass, 1984.

Helms, J. E. *Black and White Racial Identity: Theory, Research, and Practice.* Westport, Conn.: Greenwood Press, 1990.

Jackson, B. "Black Identity Development." *Journal of Educational Diversity,* 1975, *2,* 19–25.

Parham, T. A. "Cycles of Psychological Nigrescence." *The Counseling Psychologist,* 1989a, *17,* 187–226.

Parham, T. A. "Nigrescence: The Transformation of Black Consciousness Across the Life Cycle." In R. E. Jones (ed.), *Black Adult Development and Aging.* Berkeley, Calif.: Cobb and Henry, 1989b.

Parham, T. A., and Williams, P. T. "The Relationship of Demographic and Background Factors to Racial Identity Attitudes." *Journal of Black Psychology,* 1993, *19,* 7–24.

Plummer, D. L. "Patterns of Racial Identity Development of African American Adolescent Males and Females." *Journal of Black Psychology,* 1995, *21* (2), 168–180.

Pollard, D. S. "Gender, Achievement, and African American Students' Perceptions of Their School Experience." *Educational Psychologist,* 1993, *28* (4), 341–356.

Rotheram, M. J., and Phinney, J. S. "Introduction: Definitions and Perspectives in the Study of Children's Ethnic Socialization." In J. S. Phinney and M. J. Rotheram (eds.), *Children's Ethnic Socialization.* Thousand Oaks, Calif.: Sage, 1987.

Smith, E.M.J. "Black Racial Identity Development." *The Counseling Psychologist,* 1989, *17* (2), 277–288.

Strange, C. C., and King, P. M. "The Professional Practice of Student Development." In D. G. Creamer (ed.), *College Student Development.* Alexandria, Va.: American College Personnel Association, 1990.

Tatum, B. D. "Talking About Race, Learning About Racism: The Application of Racial Identity Development Theory in the Classroom." *Harvard Educational Review,* 1992, *62* (1), 1–24.

Taylor, J. "The Pittsburgh Project—Part I: Toward Community Growth and Survival." In W. E. Cross (ed.), *The Third Conference on Empirical Research in Black Psychology.* Washington, D.C.: National Institute of Education, 1976.

Thomas, C. *Boys No More.* Westerville, Ohio: Glencoe, 1971.

JANICE DAWSON-THREAT *is assistant professor of higher education and student affairs at the University of Missouri-Columbia.*

Historically, mentoring in higher education has proven to be a valuable and effective tool in promoting interaction between students and faculty. African American men in particular have reaped the benefits of formally structured mentoring programs at colleges and universities.

Retaining African American Men Through Mentoring Initiatives

Bruce D. LaVant, John L. Anderson, Joseph W. Tiggs

In recent years, institutions of higher education have placed special emphasis on recruiting students of color. Although these efforts have yielded some positive outcomes, a collective concern continues to persist that the visibility and presence of African Americans on most American campuses have not met expected goals. Additionally troublesome is that the numbers reveal enormous gender inequities in African American college populations. African American women are the primary beneficiaries of and largely responsible for the gains made by African Americans in higher education in recent years. African American men simply are not enrolling at traditionally nonblack campuses in the same proportions as African American women and their white male counterparts (Carter and Wilson, 1995).

The reasons for gender inequities are well chronicled in current research, with emphasis on the multiple challenges that African American men face in their endeavor to adjust and successfully matriculate through the traditional educational system (Harris, 1996). However, evidence also shows that when black men have been given the opportunity to participate in higher education, and when well-conceived and formalized support systems are put into place to promote achievement, black men have been successful (Harris, 1996; Morgan, 1996). Pounds (1987), Fleming (1981, 1984), Astin (1982), and Parker and Scott (1985) contend that in order to retain minority students, the campus must be responsive in its efforts to provide a warm, supportive, and nurturing environment. They argue that programs must be devised and implemented to establish an immediate connection between university personnel and students at the moment they arrive on campus.

This chapter describes how the ancient art of mentoring, one of several intervention processes that enhance retention and success, continues to be a viable alternative working in favor of the underrepresented African American male. The chapter defines the mentoring process, outlines its theoretical framework, presents mentoring approaches taken by several universities, and provides recommendations for implementing mentoring elsewhere.

The Mentoring Process Defined

Mentoring dates back to the ancient Greeks; the term is linked to Greek mythology and the character of Odysseus. The virtues of mentoring have withstood the test of time and have been found applicable to a variety of situations, including the undergraduate education experience. Jacobi states that "whereas mentoring has been long associated with an apprentice model of graduate education, it is increasingly looked upon as a retention and enrichment strategy for undergraduate education" (1991, p. 505). From the literature, she discovers a wide range of interpretations and applications of the mentoring process.

Several researchers from the higher education and business sectors have offered definitional meanings and interpretations of mentoring. For example, Shandley (1989) describes mentoring from a higher education perspective as an intentional process involving interaction between two or more individuals. He states that mentoring is a nurturing process that fosters the growth and development of the protégé. Mentoring is an insightful process in which the wisdom of the mentor is acquired and applied by the protégé. Shandley views mentoring as a supportive, oftentimes protective process. The mentor can serve as an important guide or reality checker and introduces the mentee to the environment he or she is preparing to enter. Moore and Amey (1988) define mentoring as a form of professional socialization wherein a more experienced individual acts as a guide, role model, teacher, and patron of a less experienced protégé. The aim of the relationship is to further develop and refine the young person's skills, abilities, and understanding.

Definitions specific to the business community have been cited that lend support to the importance of mentoring. Fagenson (1989) describes the mentor as someone in a position of power who gives advice or brings a protégé's accomplishments to the attention of those who have power in the company. Zey (1984) suggests that a mentor is a person who oversees the career and development of another person, usually a junior, through teaching, counseling, providing psychological support, protecting, and at times promoting or sponsoring. Lastly, Phillips-Jones (1982) observes that mentors really influence people who significantly help them reach their major life goals. Mentoring is also referred to as role modeling, which requires direct interaction between the mentor and the protégé. Understandably, the type of interaction that occurs between the mentor and mentee greatly influences the development and outcome of the mentoring relationship.

Primarily, two types of mentoring, formal and informal, are used in postsecondary education. Formal mentoring programs are designed to increase enrollment and retention of minority and other students, as well as increase student satisfaction with the academic experience (James, 1989; O'Brien, 1988; Paratore, 1984).

Informal mentoring is an ad hoc, spontaneous relationship, established by two or more individuals for the benefit of those involved. The extent to which informal mentoring is applied in higher education is unknown; however, evidence does support the notion that informal mentoring positively influences establishment of formal mentoring initiatives. Since many informal mentoring relationships are reported to promote academic success, more extensive and formally structured models have resulted following their lead (Jacobi, 1991).

Retention and Mentoring

Astin (1984) and Tinto (1993) identify several variables that contribute to student attrition. Tinto finds that academic and social integration are determinants that influence students' decisions to persist in school or drop out. He found that students arrive on campus with various built-in characteristics, including family backgrounds, precollege educational achievements, academic abilities, and other various personal attributes, all of which significantly influence rates of student persistence. Some African American male students enter college socially, educationally, and economically disadvantaged. By integrating them into the mainstream or social fabric of the institution (for example, student activities, minority leadership programs), their chances of persistence and matriculation are enhanced.

Astin (1984) stresses the importance of student participation in the mainstream of campus life. Significant involvement in campus activities might include sports, fraternal organizations, and leadership activities. Astin contends that active involvement aids the student's bonding with the institution. He also states that a highly involved student spends considerable time on campus, interacts frequently with faculty members and other students, and devotes a significant amount of time to studying. Both Astin and Tinto agree that when students bond with and to the university and develop a close relationship with peers, faculty, and staff, they are more likely to matriculate and graduate. The literature also suggests that it is often very difficult to mainstream African American men into campus life; thus, it is more important than ever to actively involve them in a formal mentoring process (O'Brien, 1988; Hughes, 1987).

Although the research on mentoring in higher education for African American men is sparse, some studies have been conducted exclusively on programs for African American students at the undergraduate and graduate levels and in which men are highlighted.

Frierson, Hargrove, and Lewis (1994) examine perceptions and attitudes of eighteen undergraduate African American students who participated in a summer research mentoring program at a large university. Their study attempts to address two questions that relate to African American undergraduates who participated in a nine-week summer research program:

1. What type of student-faculty relationships are expected for those students in formal programs?
2. What associated effects does faculty's race or gender have on the perceptions and attitudes of students of African Americans participating in "mentoring" programs?

The interview results obtained from the eleven African American women and seven African American men who participated indicate that at the completion of the program, those with black or women mentors had more positive perceptions and attitudes toward research and the research environment than those with white male mentors. Findings from this study support the perception that black faculty presence is important in providing positive attitudes toward research and academic careers in African American students.

Hoyte and Collett (1993) have conducted similar studies that focus on mentoring African American students involved in the sciences. They interviewed students who were participating in two programs established by the National Institute of Health (NIH). The Minority Biomedical Research Support (MBRS) and the Minority Access to Research Careers (MARC) programs are efforts by NIH to increase representation of minorities in the sciences. These projects provide a select group of African American students who are taking science classes with a faculty mentor in the laboratory exercises. Findings from this study suggest that close relations between the mentor and student and the presence of role models contribute to students' positive attributes.

Mentoring Models

Numerous examples exist of viable and successful college and university mentoring programs for African American students. Since the factors affecting black men's matriculation are different from those of black women, a number of these programs focus on mentoring African American men only. Four such programs are presented here. However, since many campuses are not able to afford the luxury of a mentoring program exclusively for African American men, it is important to examine a sampling of programs established for mentoring both men and women in which black men are known to benefit.

The Black Man's Think Tank. One successful mentoring program for African American men can be found at the University of Cincinnati. The program is run by Eric Abercrombie, director of the African Cultural and Research Center and the Office of Ethnic Programs and Services. Abercrombie created the Black Man's Think Tank in 1993. The Think Tank provides an arena and forum for black male academicians to discuss issues and concerns that confront black male students in higher education. As a result of their discussions, a decision was made that the Think Tank would spearhead a mentoring and leadership program matching undergraduate black male students with black male professional staff. Abercrombie explains that students often fail not because of academic reasons but because they do not know how or are unable to set priorities, balance male-female relationships, or learn to sacrifice. Emphasis is also placed on being committed to "our people" and giving back and serving as peers and mentors to younger brothers and sisters. One of Abercrombie's protégés, Lee Jones, director of the Office of Multicultural Student Services at Washington State University and assistant professor of educational leadership, states that Abercrombie has influenced the work he has done with young African American men while at Washington State University and Ohio State University. Jones also established a mentoring program at Washington State entitled 100 African American Men. It brings black male students together to address issues that affect them. African American male freshmen and transfer students are identified and assigned a male faculty mentor upon admission to WSU.

The Student African American Brotherhood (SAAB). In 1990, the Student African American Brotherhood (SAAB) was founded by Tyrone Bledsoe on the campus of Georgia Southwestern University. The organization is established to provide student development intervention and support to African American men enrolled in college; it is further designed as a black male development model. One of its goals is to assist African American men in developing a more complete understanding of their responsibilities in being U.S. citizens. Leadership development and training is also an important initiative of this organization. To accomplish its goals, educational and cultural activities are offered to all student participants. Services such as tutorial assistance, career planning and counseling, cultural and social activities, personal development opportunities, community service, and spiritual enrichments are offered. All of the programs of this organization are designed to promote positive thinking and promote high self-esteem in African American men. SAAB currently exists on three other college campuses: North Carolina Central University, the University of Texas at Austin, and Albany State University in Georgia. By offering these services, role models, and mentoring through this innovative approach, the chances for successful college matriculation for African American men are greatly enhanced.

The Black Male Initiative. In an effort to encourage black youth in inner cities to enter colleges and universities, Texas Southern University established the Black Male Initiative in 1990 to encourage black youth to continue their education. The program promotes the values of education and provides workshops and other informative events that bring successful role models to the forefront. Successful business and community leaders participate and provide inspiration to the students. The program assists students in understanding their capabilities and talents and offers them several opportunities to maximize their potential.

The Meyerhoff Program. Another example of a successful program that includes a formal mentoring component is based at the University of

Maryland, Baltimore County (UMBC). The Meyerhoff Program was created in 1988 by Freeman Hrabowski III, president of UMBC. The program's primary purpose is to increase the number of African American men who earn doctorates, and ultimately improve the number of minority college faculty in engineering, medicine, and the sciences. Because other Maryland initiatives were coming under intense legal scrutiny for discrimination, the program began admitting and offering services to African American women in 1990 and to other ethnic groups in 1996. But the primary focus is still on the issues and concerns of African American men. Hrabowski indicates that mentoring is a critical component of this program and states that "the challenge we are confronted with is creating role models of smart black males who can help other little boys to want to be like them" (Morgan, 1996, p. 17). The mentoring component offered through the Meyerhoff Program, which embraces African American men as soon as they arrive on campus, can serve as a model for other academic settings. The program identifies students early, provides appropriate role models in a supportive environment, and exposes them to other students who are like them; there is evidence that the Meyerhoff Program enhances retention of these students. For a more detailed description of the program, including the mentoring component, see Chapter Six.

The Bridge. Georgia State University initiated a program called The Bridge in the mid-1980s with the express purpose of providing a jump start at the freshman level and enrichment of experience for African American students. Mentoring is a major aspect of the program, which provides an opportunity for students, faculty, and staff to engage in one-on-one relationships. This also provides an avenue to foster relationships with African American male program participants. Many of the faculty and staff are white and serve as mentors and instructors in the program. The developers of the program report that the relationships make the students feel accepted, respected, and supported, and that it has greatly influenced and enhanced their chances for persistence and graduation. The Bridge communicates the message that education is not something that happens, but something each individual must create for himself or herself (Chapman and Logan, 1996). The Bridge is now in place on four other Georgia campuses and has helped to shape the experience, and aid in the matriculation and graduation, of African American students on these predominantly white campuses.

Project BEAM. Project BEAM (Being Excited About Me) assists students of color in gaining admission to West Virginia University and also provides academic support and other services. BEAM is predicated on the fact that establishing a one-to-one relationship with prospective students and really getting to know them establishes trust and gains student commitment, which leads to successful retention. BEAM is a strategic program at WVU, designed to improve African American students' coping abilities at predominantly white colleges and universities. BEAM's top administrators at WVU recognize that BEAM is quite different from the already established campus programs for recruitment and retention of African American students. The program matches black faculty, administrators, directors, staff employees, and individuals from the community with selected students. A mentoring task force conducts a mentor training program and evaluates its effectiveness. African American men participate in and benefit from this innovative program, which has been reported to be successful in accomplishing its goals.

The Faculty Mentor Program-University of Louisville

The University of Louisville is one of the universities that experienced a significant increase in freshman African American enrollment in the early 1980s. However, the number of black students enrolled fell off dramatically after the first year of enrollment. University administrators, faculty, and staff made assumptions about the attrition problems that are consistent with research suggesting that problematic retention is related to campus climate. They concluded that many inner-city youth come to the university from neighborhoods where their racial identity is of majority status. They walk into an environment that is less warm and welcoming, one where they are numerically in the minority. Many of these students are first-generation college students and some are from "out of town," factors that contemporary researchers equate with high risk.

In an effort to make the campus more hospitable and reach out to this underrepresented population, the Faculty Mentor Program was initiated in 1984 to enhance retention and persistence of African American students; it has since been in continuous operation. The philosophy behind the program is for an experienced and caring faculty member to assist in providing a nurturing environment, to help the student become connected with the system and feel welcomed, and to provide the kind of direction that allows optimum use of the student's talent and achievement of his or her goals. The mentor's role entails friendship, guidance, counseling, a warm and genuine smile at times, referrals, and encouragement; it also means playing student advocate, navigator, proofreader, and alarm clock as needed.

The Faculty Mentor Program at the University of Louisville assigns a faculty mentor to all African American freshmen admitted to degree-granting units. Mentors are selected from all colleges of the university, and specific assignments are made on the basis of the student's proposed major. Therefore, a common interest exists between the mentor and mentee, which facilitates the relationship. The mentor's role involves proactive contact by phone, letter, and electronic mail whenever possible, culminating in sustained bimonthly or monthly face-to-face contacts. The mentor also serves as the mentee's principal adviser. Early contacts are vital as students are greeted and introduced to the program during the summer orientation and registration period. Mentors document their contacts and continue to track the African American mentees throughout their college career and often after graduation.

Several events are scheduled throughout the year to foster high-quality relationships between mentors and mentees and also to help the mentees gain a feeling of ownership of the campus. On-campus events have included ice cream socials, pizza fests, Halloween parties, and an end-of-the-year barbecue. Free tickets are provided to concerts both on and off campus as long as both mentor and mentee attend together. Jazz week events, arranged by a mentor in the school of music, have been a tradition. Mentors and protégés also are invited to attend academic events together that may be of relevance to individual success and character building. Although student selection into the program is not based upon gender, the program is sensitive to the special needs of males. For instance, a Kentucky state senator, who was an official observer of the Republic of South Africa's first nationwide free election, addressed the group in 1995. As an African American man, the senator provided a positive role model appealing to the male portion of the mentored population. Faculty are also encouraged to tap into a special fund to provide for their own individual social events, and some have done so.

A total of 129 African American freshmen admitted to degree-granting units were accepted to participate in the mentoring program in the fall of 1994. Twenty-four African American men were identified from this group. The low proportion of men is indicative of the gender inequity mentioned earlier in this chapter. Four of the twenty-four were unresponsive to the proactive efforts by mentors and were declared inactive.

At the University of Louisville, experience has shown that when African American men are provided with opportunities to partake of the services of an institution and become connected with compassionate and knowledgeable faculty within the system, they successfully compete with their white counterparts. Actually, two-thirds of the mentored African American men were retained over the course of five regular semesters (two and one-half years), and most (nine of fourteen) achieved junior status. The results compared favorably to the 1993–94 annual retention rate of 74.9 percent at the University of Louisville.

Another example of positive results from the university's faculty mentoring program is found in the following data: in 1992, eighty-five African American students enrolled and were recipients of minority scholarships. The eighty-five were also participants in the faculty mentoring program. Twenty-nine African American men were among this group. After "tracking" this group for nine semesters, through fall 1996 (approximately four and one-half years) it was found that:

- Five of the 29 have graduated with four-year degrees and three are attending graduate schools.
- Fourteen are still matriculating and are enrolled for spring 1997.
- Cumulative hours earned range from 20 to 129.
- Average cumulative hours earned equaled 98.
- GPAs ranged from 1.6 to 3.4, with an overall average of 2.5.
- Four withdrew or did not reenroll but left in good standing and are attending other universities.

- Two withdrew or did not reenroll on warning status.
- One withdrew while on probation.
- Three were dismissed by the university.

Essentially, two-thirds of this black male cohort of the fall 1992 class graduated by fall 1996 or are continuing their education successfully, which compares favorably with the general student population.

Recommendations

Based on the observations of the faculty mentoring programs offered at several postsecondary institutions, it is recommended that in order to have a viable and effective mentoring program that promotes and enhances the retention, academic achievement, and leadership development of African American men:

- The executive leadership within the institution must be genuinely committed to the concept of a formal mentoring program.
- Resources (human and financial) must be allocated for support of the program.
- A university committee should be established to identify African American male students, upon admission, who might be potential program participants or mentees.
- Energetic, compassionate, and dedicated individuals from all fields of expertise and levels within the university must be selected as mentors.
- The program coordinator or director should work very closely with the university's admissions office and registrar to obtain information related to potential and current program participants.
- A training program must be developed for faculty and staff who are selected to serve in the program.
- External (local) community support for the program must be established by marketing it to community leaders, business affiliates, and educators.
- An unbiased assessment and evaluation of all phases of the program must be an ongoing process, since redesign can be expected and a program may be ignored or eliminated for lack of objective documentation regarding its effectiveness.

Summary

Because African American men make up only 3.9 percent of the current college enrollment (*Chronicle of Higher Education,* 1997), it is incumbent upon administrators, faculty, staff, community leaders, and parents to continue to devise strategies and implement programs that positively affect retention of these students once they arrive on college and university campuses. It is also imperative that initiatives be created to attract, encourage, and motivate the African American man who might be a potential college student but needs that extra support or attention to increase his interest and make him more comfortable with the idea of participating in postsecondary education.

Fleming (1984), Hughes (1987), Harris (1996), Woolbright (1989), and Wright (1987) observe that students who interact and become involved in a mentoring relationship find greater satisfaction in their collegiate experiences than those persons who do not have this experience. This kind of satisfaction is consistently reported and experienced by minority students, particularly African American men and professionals fortunate enough to benefit from having a mentor to advise them, teach them, and guide their efforts at crucial points in their educational, professional, and personal development.

Application of mentoring proves to be an effective tool in providing the support necessary to overcome the barriers that prevent many African American men from successfully completing college. Mentoring is vital in contributing to the survival and empowering of African American men, and it also enhances their ability to make plausible gains in the higher education milieu. Current literature asserts, and effective programs testify, that if African American men are to be successful in their pursuit of a degree in higher education, positive and creative intervention methods must be developed. Mentoring in higher education continues to assist African American men in developing and becoming role models for others.

References

Astin, A. W. *Minorities in American Higher Education: Recent Trends, Current Prospects, and Recommendations.* San Francisco: Jossey-Bass, 1982.

Astin, A. W. "Student Involvement: A Developmental Theory for Higher Education." *Journal of College Student Personnel,* 1984, *25,* 287–300.

Carter, D. J., and Wilson, R. "Minorities in Education." In *Fourteenth Annual Status Report.* Washington, D.C.: American Council on Education, 1995.

Chapman, C. A., and Logan, B. L. "The Bridge: A Viable Retention Program for African-American Students." In C. A. Ford (ed.), *Student Retention Success Models in Higher Education.* Tallahassee, Fla.: CNJ Associates, 1996.

Chronicle of Higher Education, Aug. 29, 1997 (in vol. 44, no. 1), p. 18.

Fagenson, E. A. "The Mentor Advantage: Perceived Career/Job Experiences of Protégés Versus Non-Protégés." *Journal of Organizational Behavior,* 1989, *10,* 309–320.

Fleming, J. E. "The Opening of White Colleges and Universities to Black Students." In G. E. Thomas (ed.), *Black Students in Higher Education: Conditions and Experiences in the 1970s.* Westport, Conn.: Greenwood Press, 1981.

Fleming, J. *Blacks in College: A Comparative Study of Students' Success in Black and in White Institutions.* San Francisco: Jossey-Bass, 1984.

Frierson, H. T., Hargrove, B. K., and Lewis, N. R. "Black Summer Research Students' Perceptions Related to Research Mentors' Race and Gender." *Journal of College Student Development,* 1994, *35* (6), 475–480.

Harris, W. G. "African-American Males in Higher Education: Reframing the Issue." *Black Issues in Higher Education,* Oct. 3, 1996, pp. 13, 16, 92.

Hoyte, R. M., and Collett, J. C. "I Can Do It: Minority Undergraduate Science Experiences and the Professional Career Choice." In J. Gainen and R. Boice (eds.), *Building a Diverse Faculty.* New Directions for Teaching and Learning, no. 53. San Francisco: Jossey-Bass, 1993, pp. 81–92.

Hughes, M. "Black Students' Participation in Higher Education." *Journal of College Student Personnel*, 1987, *28*, 532.

Jacobi, M. "Mentoring and Undergraduate Academic Success: A Literature Review." *Review of Educational Research*, 1991, *61* (4), 505–532.

James, D. P. "Increasing Retention Rates of Black Students." *Mentoring International*, 1989, *3* (2), 34–39.

Moore, K. M., and Amey, M. J. "Some Faculty Leaders Are Born Women." In M.A.D. Sagaria (ed.), *Empowering Women: Leadership Development Strategies on Campus*. New Directions for Student Services, no. 44. San Francisco: Jossey-Bass, 1988.

Morgan, J. "Reaching Out to Young Black Men." *Black Issues in Higher Education*, 1996, *92*, 16–19.

O'Brien, E. "Dr. Charles Willis Prescribes Mentoring Methodologies for Minorities." *Black Issues in Higher Education*, 1988, *5* (5), 15.

Paratore, J. "The Relationship Between Participation in a Mentoring Program and Developmental Growth and Persistence of Freshman Students at Southern Illinois University at Carbondale." Unpublished doctoral dissertation, Southern Illinois University, Carbondale, 1984.

Parker, W. P., and Scott, A. C. "Creating an Inviting Atmosphere for College Students for Ethnic Minority Groups." *Journal of College Student Personnel*, 1985, *26* (1), 82–87.

Phillips-Jones, L. *Mentors and Protégés*. New York: Arbor House, 1982.

Pounds, A. W. "Black Students' Needs on Predominantly White Campuses." In D. J. Wright (ed.), *Responding to the Needs of Today's Minority Students*. New Directions for Student Services, no. 38. San Francisco: Jossey-Bass, 1987.

Shandley, T. C. "The Use of Mentors for Leadership Development." *NASPA Journal*, 1989, *27*, 59–66.

Tinto, V. *Leaving College: Rethinking the Causes and Cures of Student Attrition*. Chicago: University of Chicago Press, 1993.

Woolbright, C. *Valuing Diversity on Campus: A Multicultural Approach*. Bloomington, Ind.: Association of College Unions-International, 1989.

Wright, D. "Minority Students: Developmental Beginnings." In D. J. Wright (ed.), *Responding to the Needs of Today's Minority Students*. New Directions for Student Services, no. 38. San Francisco: Jossey-Bass, 1987.

Zey, M. G. *The Mentor Connection*. Homewood, Ill.: Dow Jones-Irwin, 1984.

BRUCE D. LAVANT *is director of the Division of Transitional Studies and adjunct professor of educational and counseling psychology at the University of Louisville.*

JOHN L. ANDERSON *is coordinator of the Faculty Mentoring Program and assistant professor of geography and geosciences at the University of Louisville.*

JOSEPH W. TIGGS *is a doctoral student in the Department of Educational and Counseling Psychology at the University of Louisville.*

_vide greater leadership involvement among African American men within campuswide organizations, student affairs professionals must articulate clearly the advantages of becoming leaders. In addition, institutions should seek avenues to empower black male leadership, particularly within fraternities, which would increase greater involvement throughout campuswide organizations.

Identifying and Developing Leadership Opportunities for African American Men

E. Michael Sutton, Melvin C. Terrell

Student populations on our campuses are becoming increasingly more diverse. Within the last twenty years, the racial makeup of students has changed significantly (Fleming, 1984). Consequently, student affairs professionals should remain advocates of promoting an environment that is conducive for all students to participate and assume leadership positions within campuswide organizations.

However, minority students attending predominantly white institutions still encounter difficulty adjusting to campus life academically and socially. According to Parker and Scott (1985), Astin (1982), and Fleming (1981, 1984) many students of color perceive the climate at predominantly white campuses as hostile. These negative perceptions may influence many African American men not to participate as leaders within campuswide organizations. Although membership in these organizations is open, many minority students continue to perceive them as unwelcoming. Loo and Rolison (1986) indicate that feelings of social and cultural isolation contribute to diminished leadership opportunities among African American students. These sentiments may inhibit ethnic minority student involvement within campuswide organizations other than their own.

Although the literature addresses African American student leadership in general (DeSousa and King, 1992; Wright, 1987; Rooney, 1985; and Harper, 1975), little research has been conducted identifying and developing leadership opportunities among African American men. Therefore, this chapter presents the benefits to African American men of leadership participation within

NEW DIRECTIONS FOR STUDENT SERVICES, no. 80, Winter 1997 © Jossey-Bass Publishers student organizations, as well as discussing the opportunities minority student groups and black fraternities contribute to African American male leadership. In conclusion, the findings of a study examining African American men's perceptions of available leadership opportunities within campuswide organizations are shared.

Opportunities for Leadership

According to Rooney (1985) and Schuh and Laverty (1983), leadership involvement in campuswide organizations prepares students for the realities of civil, political, and social life upon graduation. These intangible skills are beneficial to students involved not only in campus governance activities but in other organizations as well. Participation in student government is an excellent opportunity to develop leadership skills, but other campus activities provide unique leadership experiences for students also. Chambers and Phelps (1993) report that positions as resident advisers, peer counselors, and representatives to institutional governing bodies provide meaningful opportunities for students to develop leadership skills. Although these leadership opportunities are available to all students, few African American men are represented or involved. According to LaVant and Terrell (1994), the lack of ethnic minority participation in student government is related to their low participation in similar experiences during high school. In addition, low participation among African American students is attributed to their perceptions that student governance and campuswide organization issues are not relevant to their personal collegiate experiences (Willie and McCord, 1972). Consequently, many African American men choose to develop their leadership skills within the African American community rather than campuswide organizations (Harper, 1975).

Programs that involve students as mentors provide an additional opportunity for African American men to participate as campus leaders. Realizing that minority retention is a major issue, institutions that recruit and train African American men as peer mentors not only enhance minority retention but increase the visibility of African American men as leaders. According to Shandley (1989), students involved in this unique leadership experience become role models, guides, and confidants to new and transfer students while developing their own leadership skills. Consequently, if African American men are to assume greater leadership positions within campuswide organizations, they must feel their contributions as leaders are valued (Williams, 1987; Pascarella and Terenzini, 1991). However, Krumbein (1989) cautioned that empowerment of minority students is beneficial only when they are allowed to participate in meaningful decision-making dialogue.

Minority Student Group Leadership

Many African American students who are not involved as leaders within campuswide organizations choose to develop their leadership experiences through minority student groups. Organizations such as Black Student Unions, Black ssociations, and the Black Gospel Choir develop minority students' ___onal and planning skills and also enhance their aptitudes of self-_____, __dependence, and autonomy (Rooney, 1985). Although these organizations equip African American students with valuable leadership skills, they also serve as social networks and support systems within the university (DeSousa and King, 1992; Rooney, 1985; and Fleming, 1984). However, the debate goes on as to whether these organizations promote separatism and limit African American student involvement within campuswide organizations. Chevez (1982) reports that African American students attending predominantly white institutions did not prefer to participate in activities sponsored by minority student groups. In contrast, Barol and others (1983) found that minority students did prefer involvement with their own cultural groups and generally did not participate in campuswide organizations.

The preference of any African American men who participate as leaders within minority student groups could be related to their racial identity and attitude. Mitchell and Dell (1992) found that as students become more comfortable with their racial identity, they are more likely to display interest and openness in both cultural and noncultural activities. Therefore, it is advantageous for campuses to promote minority student organizations as alternatives to campuswide organizations in developing leadership skills among those African Americans whose racial identity development is not at a level permitting them to participate comfortably in campuswide groups.

Minority student groups on predominantly white campuses also serve as a catalyst for integrating African American male leaders within campuswide organizations. One should not assume these organizations discourage black student participation within campuswide organizations; rather, they provide a less intimidating environment where leadership skills can be learned. Consequently, advisers to minority student groups should increase collaborative interaction with leaders of campuswide organizations in planning campus events and programs. Through collaborative interaction, African American men become comfortable in assuming leadership positions within campuswide organizations.

Greek Leadership

Although various minority student groups provide leadership opportunities for African American men, the black fraternity remains the most popular avenue for black men to exercise leadership on predominantly white campuses. According to McKenzie (1990), black Greek organizations were created to provide leadership for the African American race while at the same time incorporating aspects of racial identification and cultural heritage. Despite negative reports of hazing and pledging, these organizations continue to recruit large numbers of African American men into their ranks.

In comparison to campuswide organizations, black fraternities provide early opportunities for black men to assume positions of leadership (Hughes and Winston, 1987). Black fraternities also enhance leadership skills of assertiveness, task completion, community service, and campus planning for their members (Striffolino and Saunders, 1989). Kimbrough (1995) found that two-thirds of black Greek men surveyed indicated that their leadership skills were enhanced through fraternity involvement. The respondents also indicated that leadership participation in campus activities was a salient skill for all African American students to learn. Since Kimbrough's results indicate that African American men perceive that participation as campus leaders is important, student affairs professionals should develop strategies to increase African American male membership and leadership in campuswide organizations.

Schuh, Triponey, Heim, and Nishimura (1992) suggest student affairs professionals should increase their knowledge of black Greek organizations and recognize their leadership contributions throughout the campus community. Through campus and community recognition, African American men realize that their leadership contributions and values are embraced by the total campus community. Student affairs professionals should also encourage increased collaboration between black male Greeks and leaders of campuswide organizations in planning social events such as homecoming and Greek Week. This positive interaction promotes camaraderie and cultural understanding of both organizations' leadership contributions.

Finally, student affairs practitioners should provide greater monetary support to assist African American male leaders in attending professional leadership conferences such as the National Pan-Hellenic Council (NPHC). These professional experiences not only enhance African American men's understanding of leadership development but provide opportunities to interact with other African American male leaders and mentors (Schuh, Triponey, Heim, and Nishimura, 1992).

A Study of Leadership Perceptions Among African American Men

Previous studies concerning minority student leadership at predominantly white institutions have focused upon levels of involvement between black and white students within campuswide organizations (DeSousa and King, 1992) and black student involvement within minority support organizations (Rooney, 1985). An additional study by Kimbrough (1995) examined the views of members of black Greek organizations and their role in leadership development. Furthermore, Schuh, Triponey, Heim, and Nishimura (1992) examined student involvement in historically black organizations at a large midwestern university. Although those studies describe minority student leadership in general, the purpose of the current research was to assess directly African American men's perceptions of leadership and the availability of these opportunities at predominantly white campuses.

Methodology. A four-part questionnaire was developed by student affairs and assessment professionals at one of the two institutions being studied to ascertain demographic information, fraternity leadership involvement, and respondents' perceptions of opportunities for leadership for African American men attending a predominantly white campus. Subjects were asked to respond to five open-ended questions regarding methods their campuses can use to improve leadership opportunities for African American men. The African American Greek male population at the two institutions chosen for this study included eighty members.

Results. The findings from this research indicate that African American men who are leaders within their fraternities are also involved in campuswide organizations. Twenty-seven (49.1 percent) held one or two leadership positions outside their fraternity, while thirty-six (65.5 percent) indicated they were somewhat involved within campuswide organizations. A correlation coefficient of .529 indicated a strong relationship between leadership positions held by African American fraternity men and their level of involvement in campuswide organizations.

Participants were asked to report the type of organization in which black men received their primary leadership experience; twenty (36.4 percent) agreed or strongly agreed that predominantly black organizations developed their initial leadership skills. When asked whether black men fail to assume leadership positions in campuswide organizations because they perceive the organizations as unwelcoming, twenty-five (45.5 percent) agreed while fifteen (27.3 percent) strongly agreed with this statement. Consequently, African American male leaders indicate that the minority support organizations on the campuses, such as BSA, BSU, and Gospel Choir, provided them with their initial leadership experiences prior to leadership within their fraternity.

The subjects also responded whether or not they received adequate leadership training prior to assuming an office within their fraternity. Of the total respondents, twenty-seven (49.1 percent) disagreed, indicating that they were not adequately trained, while fourteen (25.5 percent) agreed they were prepared to assume leadership positions within their fraternity. However, when asked whether black men fail to assume leadership in campuswide organizations because of lack of leadership training sponsored by the institution, twenty-two (40 percent) disagreed that the institution is responsible for providing training programs for leaders.

A correlation coefficient of .314 was significant, indicating a strong relationship between black men's perceptions of being adequately trained prior to assuming office and whether lack of leadership training inhibits leadership participation among black men within campuswide organizations. Therefore, the majority of the subjects reported they are inadequately trained for the leadership positions they currently hold but did not perceive participating in leadership training programs sponsored by the institution as a benefit to assuming leadership roles within campuswide organizations.

The researchers developed five open-ended questions to ascertain the respondents' perceptions of how fraternity membership influenced leadership activity in campuswide organizations regarding leadership participation and involvement. The responses for each question are summarized below.

Question 1. *What impact, if any, has being involved in a fraternity had in encouraging you to become a student leader?*

The majority of the respondents indicated that their fraternity provided them with confidence and leadership skills, such as time management and responsibility, to assume leadership positions outside their fraternity. Many credit their organizations for surfacing their hidden leadership qualities and strengthening their organizational and people skills. Members also perceived that their fraternal involvement encouraged them to assume leadership positions within the African American community. However, some members indicated their fraternity involvement has not helped or has been of little help in encouraging African American men to assume student leadership.

Question 2. *Please describe the leadership positions you have held on campus.*

Overwhelmingly, the respondents indicated they did not hold any leadership position within campuswide organizations. The majority indicated they held leadership positions as officers, such as president, secretary, sergeant at arms, or treasurer, only within their fraternities. A few reported involvement in the Interfraternity Council, Student Government Association, and Circle K. It should be noted that those men who were involved in campuswide organizations did not hold any leadership position within these organizations.

Question 3. *Who on your campus do you perceive as a role model? What impact has the individual had on your leadership development?*

The respondents consistently viewed African American professional staff members (directors of minority affairs, admissions staff, and academic advisers) as role models on their campuses. A few perceived their minister or a white faculty member as a role model. A small number indicated that peers who had graduated and were pursuing graduate and professional degrees served as role models.

Question 4. *What can your campus do to encourage black males to become involved in major student organizations?*

A great number of the respondents suggested the university organize and provide activities that are of interest to black men. Many of the respondents requested activities, seminars, and lectures that promote unity among African American men.

Several men suggested the university sponsor more multicultural programs that would promote a friendlier campus environment among their white counterparts. One respondent suggested a dialogue should occur between African American and white students regarding the benefits black men gain by being involved in majority organizations.

Finally, several respondents indicated the institution should recognize the contributions of African American male leadership on campus by soliciting their advice and supporting their programs.

Question 5. *Please describe the types of on-campus or off-campus leadership education in which you have been involved (such as leadership development programs, classroom instruction, workshops and seminars).*

Many of the respondents were involved in general leadership seminars or workshops prior to their college experience. It appears the community involved these men in leadership programs such as "InRoads," the Masonic Order, and the YMCA. It is noted with interest that black men did not credit their institutions for providing leadership training programs. In addition, many of the black men surveyed choose to share their leadership talents with agencies within the African American community. Several fraternity members serve as tutors and mentors for inner-city youth at the local YMCA or Boys Club. Also, several are leaders within their youth groups or church school.

Discussion. The findings of this research reveal encouraging news regarding black male participation within campuswide organizations. These data indicate that black men who hold leadership positions within their fraternities are involved as members within campuswide organizations. Also, black men who are leaders within their fraternities also perceive themselves as leaders among the African American student population. This validates Kimbrough's findings (1995) that members of black Greek organizations on predominantly white campuses perceive themselves as leaders.

This study also reveals that minority support groups provide African American men with their initial leadership experience at predominantly white campuses. These data also indicate that black men perceive the climate within white-dominated groups as less supportive for learning leadership development skills. Previous research conducted by Rooney (1985) and Barol and others (1983) mirrors these findings.

A salient point of this research is that African American men recognize the need for leadership training programs for fraternity officers. Although many black men are eager to assume positions of leadership, a number indicate they are not prepared to provide the leadership needed for their organizations. Because of their unfamiliarity with specific leadership techniques (such as following parliamentary procedures, developing an agenda, and presiding at meetings) black male involvement in campuswide organizations is generally limited to nonleader membership. It is interesting to note that a majority of the respondents in this study attribute the low level of leadership participation among African American men in campuswide organizations to the institution's lack of providing leadership development programs. These findings concur with those of LaVant and Terrell (1994) and Kimbrough (1995) that African American men perceive leadership training as an important skill and desire the institution to provide programs to enhance their leadership skills.

Summary

Participation in campuswide organizations provides students with leadership skills that enhance their experiences upon graduation. Although numerous campuswide organizations provide opportunities for students to develop their leadership skills, many African American men choose to have their leadership experiences within black fraternities and minority support organizations.

The results from our study have several implications regarding black male leadership participation within campuswide organizations and how student affairs administrators can affect it. Primarily, institutions should embrace the unique yet effective roles African American men assume as community leaders by sponsoring tutorial and recreational programs for African American youth. These efforts should be recognized by the campus and the community at large with tangible rewards. Consequently, the criteria used for rewarding leadership contributions to the campus and community should be inclusive to reflect the philosophy and community service programs of black fraternities. Through campus and community recognition, black fraternity leaders perceive that the campus values inclusion, fairness, and sharing of power. As previously stated, collaboration between African American male Greek leaders and leaders of campuswide organizations promote positive dialogue and cultural appreciation of the diverse styles of leadership that both groups contribute to the campus. If African American male leaders perceive that their contributions as leaders are valued by the total campus community, many will choose to participate as leaders outside their traditional ethnic organizations.

Subsequently, institutions must provide greater fiscal and moral support to social events and educational programs sponsored by minority student organizations. These organizations can certainly play a vital role in developing organizational and planning skills of black men in conjunction with their black Greek experience. Advisers to minority support organizations should provide opportunities for minority leaders to interact with other leaders from majority campus organizations. This interaction not only promotes unity among black and white student leaders but also provides regular and consistent communication between them regarding leadership styles and skills. In particular, collaboration between African American male Greek leaders and leaders of campuswide organizations promotes positive dialogue and cultural appreciation of the diverse styles of leadership both groups contribute to the campus.

Both campus administrators and Greek chapter advisers should seek more opportunities to provide comprehensive leadership training programs for fraternity officers. These sessions provide black men with important leadership skills and also instill a level of comfort and confidence that facilitates an easier transition to leadership positions within campuswide organizations.

References

Astin, A. W. *Minorities in American Higher Education: Recent Trends, Current Prospects, and Recommendations.* San Francisco: Jossey-Bass, 1982.

Astin, A. W. "Student Involvement: A Developmental Theory for Higher Education." *Journal of College Student Personnel,* 1984, *26,* 297–308.

Astin, A. W. *Achieving Educational Excellence: A Critical Assessment of Priorities and Practices in Higher Education.* San Francisco: Jossey-Bass, 1985.

Barol, B., Camper, D., Pigott, C., Nadolsky, R., and Sarris, M. "Separate Tables: Why White and Black Students Choose to Segregate." *Newsweek on Campus,* March 1983, pp. 4–11.

Chambers, T., and Phelps, C. E. "Student Activism as a Form of Leadership and Student Development." *NASPA Journal,* 1993, *31* (1), 19–29.

Chevez, E. "Minority Student Involvement in Student Activities." *Association of College Unions International Bulletin,* Aug. 1982, pp. 15–16.

DeSousa, D. J., and King, P. M. "Are White Students Really More Involved in Collegiate Experiences Than Black Students?" *Journal of College Student Development,* 1992, *33,* 363–369.

Fleming, J. "Special Needs of Blacks and Other Minorities." In A. W. Chickering and Associates, *The Modern American College: Responding to the New Realities of Diverse Students and a Changing Society.* San Francisco: Jossey-Bass, 1981.

Fleming, J. *Blacks in College: A Comparative Study of Students' Success in Black and White Institutions.* San-Francisco: Jossey-Bass, 1984.

Harper, F. D. *Black Students: White Campus.* Washington, D.C.: APGA Press, 1975.

Hughes, M. J., and Winston Jr., R. B., "Effects of Fraternity Membership on Interpersonal Values." *Journal of College Student Personnel,* 1987, *28* (5), 405–411.

Kimbrough, W. M. "Self-Assessment, Participation, and Value of Leadership Skills, Activities, and Experiences for Black Students Relative to Their Membership in Historically Black Fraternities and Sororities." *Journal of Negro Education,* 1995, *64* (1), 63–74.

Krumbein, G. "Student Leadership Groups at the Middle Level: Turning a School Around." *NASSP Bulletin,* 1989, *73,* 40–45.

LaVant, B. D., and Terrell, M. C. "Assessing Ethnic Minority Student Leadership and Involvement in Student Government." In M. C. Terrell and M. J. Cuyjet (eds.), *Developing Student Government Leadership.* New Directions for Student Services, no. 66. San Francisco: Jossey-Bass, 1994.

Loo, C. M., and Rolison, G. "Alienation of Ethnic Minority Students at a Predominantly White University." *Journal of Higher Education,* 1986, *57,* 58–77.

McKenzie, A. "Community Service and Social Action: Using the Past to Guide the Future of Black Greek-Letter Fraternities." *NASPA Journal,* 1990, *28* (1), 30–36.

Mitchell, M. L., and Dell, D. M. "The Relationship Between Black Students' Racial Identity Attitude and Participation in Campus Organizations." *Journal of College Student Development,* 1992, *33,* 39–43.

Parker, W. M., and Scott, J. "Creating an Inviting Atmosphere for College Students from Ethnic Minority Groups." *Journal of College Student Personnel,* 1985, *26,* 82–84.

Pascarella, E. T., and Terenzini, P. T. *How College Affects Students: Findings and Insights from Twenty Years of Research.* San Francisco: Jossey-Bass, 1991.

Rooney, G. W. "Minority Students' Involvement in Minority Student Organizations: An Exploratory Study." *Journal of College Student Personnel,* 1985, *26* (5), 450–456.

Schuh, J. H., and Laverty, M. "The Perceived Long-Term Influence of Holding a Significant Student Leadership Position." *Journal of College Student Personnel,* 1983, *24* (1), 28–32.

Schuh, J. H., Triponey, V. L., Heim, L. L., and Nishimura, K. "Student Involvement in Historically Black Greek Letter Organizations." *NASPA Journal,* 1992, *29* (4), 274–282.

Shandley, T. C. "The Use of Mentors for Leadership Development." *NASPA Journal,* 1989, *27* (1), 59–66.

Striffolino, P., and Saunders, S. "Emerging Leaders: Students in Need of Development." *NASPA Journal,* 1989, *27* (1), 51–58.

Williams, D. J. "Minority Students: Developmental Beginnings." In D. J. Wright (ed.), *Responding to the Needs of Today's Minority Students.* New Directions for Student Services, no. 38. San Francisco: Jossey-Bass, 1987.

Willie, C. V., and McCord, A. S. *Black Students at White Colleges.* New York: Praeger, 1972.
Wright, D. J. (ed.). *Responding to the Needs of Today's Minority Students.* New Directions for Student Services, no. 38. San Francisco: Jossey-Bass, 1987.

E. *MICHAEL SUTTON is assistant professor of educational leadership and policies at the University of South Carolina, Columbia.*

MELVIN C. *TERRELL is vice president for student affairs and professor of counselor education at Northeastern Illinois University.*

Research on African American students has disproportionately focused on failure and underachievement. Gifted and talented black students and their concerns have been neglected in the literature. This chapter explores the needs, challenges, and problems encountered by gifted African American men.

Identifying and Supporting Gifted African American Men

Sharon Fries-Britt

The images created of black men in our society often confine them to environments shaped by drugs, crime, athletics, and academic failure. In education, we have contributed to this negative portrait by the disproportionate amount of research that emphasizes remediation and disadvantage. By no means is this author suggesting that research on underachievers be halted. Understanding the experiences of underachievers is critical, and researchers must continue to pursue this line of inquiry. However, the community of black collegians is diverse and multifaceted.

This chapter examines the unique challenges faced by a segment of the black male population that is rarely discussed: that of the gifted and talented black man. The chapter sets the context by first understanding how giftedness is defined and the status of research on gifted minorities. It examines the factors that affect their academic experience, identifies important issues for retaining them in college, and concludes by introducing and outlining the components of a program that has been successful in meeting their needs.

Defining Giftedness

The challenge involved in defining the concept of "giftedness" is compounded by complex factors of gender, race, culture, ethnicity and socioeconomic status. Societies have always been fascinated with those of its members whose capabilities exceed the norms. In fact, giftedness is a reflection of what society believes itself to be; consequently, it changes over time (Sternberg and Davidson, 1986). Definitions of giftedness vary tremendously and often create considerable debate. Traditional definitions of giftedness regard cognitive measures

NEW DIRECTIONS FOR STUDENT SERVICES, no. 80, Winter 1997 © Jossey-Bass Publishers

65

and objective criteria, such as intelligence tests, as primary indicators of ability; this is evidenced by the pioneering work of Terman (1925) and Hollingworth (1942), who used the Stanford-Binet Intelligence Test.

As the literature on giftedness evolved, contemporary definitions have embraced a wide range of capacities including intellectual, artistic, creative, and leadership ability (Sternberg and Davidson, 1986; Ford and Harris, 1990). Howard Gardner's theory of multiple intelligence (1983) reflects this new direction. The theory included seven areas of intelligence: linguistic, spatial, logical-mathematical, bodily-kinesthetic, musical, interpersonal, and intrapersonal. Renzulli's "three ring" conception of giftedness (1986) is yet another example. According to Renzulli, "giftedness consists of the interaction among three basic clusters of human traits—the clusters being above-average general abilities, high levels of task commitment, and high levels of creativity. Gifted and talented children are those possessing or capable of developing this composite set of traits and applying them to any potentially valuable area of human performance" (1986, p. 73). Historically, the federal government has played a major role in defining giftedness (Ford, 1996). The most recent definition demonstrates an attempt to be much more inclusive. As cited in Ford, the federal government's 1993 definition of giftedness states: "Children or youth with outstanding talent perform or show the potential for performing at remarkably high levels of accomplishment when compared with others of their age, experience, or environment. These children and youth exhibit high performance capacity in intellectual, creative, and/or artistic areas, and unusual leadership capacity, or excel in specific academic fields. They require services or activities not ordinarily provided by the schools. Outstanding talents are present in children and youth from all cultural groups, across all economic strata, and in all areas of human endeavor" (1996, p. 10).

In her own work, Ford has been instrumental in expanding the notions that giftedness is a multidimensional concept that must employ multimodal assessments. Ford argues that "such unidimensional instruments as intelligence and achievement tests do not reliably measure a multidimensional construct like intelligence, but multidimensional assessment can increase the probability of doing so (p. 32)." Assessment of giftedness should include both quantitative and qualitative strategies to assist gifted programs and selection processes in becoming more inclusive of potentially gifted students, particularly those from underrepresented groups, Ford argues. The definitions of gifted adult have also lacked consensus. It is likely that some adults with high IQs were identified as gifted as children (Piirto, 1994). But many adults show high ability later in life through their outstanding achievements. Recognition of adult talent and giftedness is to some extent easier to attribute because as adults they already have a proven track record of success in their profession or other areas of expertise.

In spite of the effort to expand the definition of giftedness to be more inclusive and responsive to cultural and social context, society continues to operate from an assumption that legitimate forms of giftedness are measured primarily by cognitive intelligence and ability and calculated by standardized tests such as the Scholastic Aptitude Test and the Graduate Record Examination.

The Status of Research on Gifted Minorities

Coupled with the complexity of defining giftedness is the literature's imbalance and neglect of understanding the needs of gifted minority populations. The majority of research on intelligence is conducted on the white middle class; research on gifted minorities in general and gifted blacks in particular is insufficient. Ford and Harris (1990) report that of the 4,109 articles found since 1924, only 2 percent, or 75 articles, addressed minority group members. If one counted only the articles addressing blacks, the percentage would be even lower. The studies on gifted minorities examine a wide range of issues and themes: improving identification of gifted minorities (Masten, 1985; Ford and Harris, 1990; Hadaway and Marek-Schroer, 1992), creating multidimensional assessments (Ford, 1996; Hadaway and Marek-Schroer, 1992), underrepresentation of minorities in honors programs (Harvey, 1986), psychosocial adjustment issues (Colangelo, 1985; Fries-Britt, 1994; Yong; 1994), and the role of parents (Hrabowski, 1991; Ford, 1995). The majority of the studies conducted on gifted blacks and other minorities exist almost exclusively at the elementary, junior high, and high school levels. Studies on gifted black collegians and gifted adults of color are almost nonexistent and are likely to be considered in studies on adult giftedness (Fries-Britt, 1994; Kitano, 1994/1995).

Given the paucity of literature on gifted blacks in general, understanding the specific needs of gifted black men, especially those in college, poses a real challenge. Inferences must be drawn from the general literature on the gifted, studies conducted on precollege populations of blacks, and the limited studies conducted to date on gifted black men in college.

Understanding the Experiences of Gifted Black Men

Many of the experiences of gifted black men mirror those that all students have. They encounter the problems associated with adjusting academically and socially to the college environment. They come from very diverse cultural, social, and economic backgrounds. They have concerns just as other students do about choice of major and career opportunities (Kerr and Colangelo, 1988). Many of these students are highly successful, ambitious, and able to accomplish impressive academic and personal goals during their collegiate careers. Unlike white students, black students are likely to face racial hostility and stereotypes more frequently.

Within the larger community of African American students, too, they share many similarities. Nevertheless, because of their identification as "gifted," they have unique experiences that warrant individual attention. Many of the experiences that gifted African American men have are shaped by factors within the African American community as well as factors outside of the community.

Peer Pressure. One of the most prevalent themes in the literature for gifted black students is peer pressure (Lindstrom and Van Sant, 1986; Fordham and Ogbu, 1986; Ford, 1996, Fries-Britt, 1994; Harvey, 1986; Baldwin, 1991). Gifted African American students are often accused by their peers of "acting white" (George, 1986; Fordham, 1988; Fordham and Ogbu, 1986). Behaviors associated with academic excellence and intellectual pursuits have historically been linked to whites, particularly the white middle class. More recently, members of Pacific Islander groups have been classified as having strong academic habits and high intelligence, even higher than those of whites. An unfavorable image has often been projected about African American and Hispanic or Latino intelligence. One need only look at the recent publication and public response to the book *The Bell Curve* (Herrnstein and Murray, 1994) to see examples of the latest attack and genetic explanation of cognitive ability by group—including poor whites (Banks, 1995). Fordham and Ogbu argue that black students' ambivalence with academic effort and success and the concept of acting white "rose partly because white Americans traditionally refused to acknowledge that black Americans are capable of intellectual achievement, and partly because black Americans subsequently began to doubt their own intellectual ability, began to define academic success as white people's prerogative, and began to discourage their peers, perhaps unconsciously, from emulating white people in academic striving, i.e., from acting white" (1986, p. 177). The express purpose of this chapter limits the extent to which we can explore the deep social, cultural, and political roots of intelligence and the construction of race and racial practices in this country; nevertheless, it is important to note that both of these concepts have complicated origins that dramatically impact the educational attainment and achievements of all groups, most notably African Americans. With these limited observations, it is easy to understand why the community of African Americans may not be associated with giftedness; hence the assumption that one is acting white.

Establishing peer group connections for gifted blacks can be difficult as they seek to find other students who share their interest and level of ambition. For black men, there are considerable social pressures to fit in with other black men and to be perceived by peers as having respect. Academic excellence and high achievement have not been reinforced as positive characteristics as often as such other skills as athletic ability. Once friendships have been forged, high-ability black students have expressed concern for leaving friends behind as they move more quickly socially and educationally (Cooley, Cornell, and Lee, 1991).

Self-Concept and Racial Identity. Research conducted on younger populations of gifted minority students indicates that they exhibit a strong sense of self and tend to adjust better socially, emotionally, and intellectually than their less-talented peers. Compared to other average students, they demonstrate higher levels of self-concept (Chiu, 1990; Kitano, 1990; Yong, 1994). In a study that compared the self-concept measures of African Americans, Mexican Americans, and Chinese Americans, Yong (1994) found that African Americans were the highest scorers on self-concept (p. 193). Although general self-concept issues for blacks are high early in their development, a growing body of literature reveals that racial identity development for gifted blacks is more complicated as they move into adolescence and beyond (Fordham, 1988;

Ford and Harris, 1991; and Cooley, Cornell, and Lee, 1991). According to Cooley, Cornell, and Lee (1991), gifted black students must "integrate in their self-concept both their racial identity as black and issues surrounding their identification labeling as gifted" (p. 166). It should be no surprise, given the accusation of acting white, to learn that gifted black students may struggle with issues of racial identity. Integration of race and giftedness is often a real challenge. Cooley, Cornell, and Lee found that "because academic achievement and giftedness are often associated with the majority culture, high ability black students may face a dilemma in trying to reconcile their abilities with their minority status. As a result, it may be difficult for high ability black students to think of themselves as both 'gifted' and black. Placement in a predominantly white gifted program could compound this problem, if it strengthens the black students' perception that there is an intrinsic association between giftedness and majority race" (1991, p. 166). Ford, Harris, and Schuerger (1993) also confirm that racial identity might be complicated for gifted black students as they strive to manage the social, cultural, and psychological factors affecting gifted blacks.

The Role of the Parents. Educators have long understood that parental involvement in education leads to higher levels of achievement. For gifted black students, the findings are no different. Studies have consistently found that family background and parental influence serve as primary forces in determining achievement over time. In precollege environments, black parents have been concerned about how schools have treated their children, from teaching and interaction with students to mislabeling them as troublemakers rather than gifted (Ford, 1995). Counselors who work with the parents and families of gifted students should not assume that they are knowledgeable and comfortable about the gifted programs (Colangelo, 1985). Many of these parents have not had much experience with gifted programs given the low numbers of minority enrollments. As parents become more informed about the purpose of gifted programs, they are more supportive and willing to have their student participate. In a study of gifted black collegians, Hrabowski found that the role of the mother was critical: "whether the family has a single parent or two parents, students view the mother's role as crucial to their success. These strong, assertive, and sometimes even pushy mothers have been consistently involved with the students' schools and their schoolwork. At least half of the mothers can talk about times when counselors advised their children to take courses lower than the level the mother considered appropriate" (1991, p. 199).

Counseling Needs. Balancing the factors of peer pressure, racial identity, and self-concept points to the need for support through counseling. In studies of precollege gifted minorities, the counseling needs are different from those of other gifted students (Colangelo, 1985). Identifying three areas that counselors should consider when working with this population (issues of identification, families, and gifted students' ethnic identity formation), Colangelo asserts that "counselors need to recognize the ambivalence these youngsters have concerning their identification and must work to provide them with a clear understanding of their abilities" (1985, p. 34). Older gifted black students may need help in sorting through their feelings of moving up in socioeconomic status. Some researchers have noted that there is emotional turmoil and conflict experienced by blacks who struggle with accepting their upward mobility and possible loss of cultural community connections as a result of being defined as gifted (Lindstrom and Van Sant, 1986). Working through the issues of succeeding in the larger society and remaining connected to their cultural community may best be handled by a counselor of their own racial group. Majority counselors can fortify good relationships with gifted blacks. However, they must be aware of their own limitations in comprehending the complex issues of social and cultural understandings, and when their training in multicultural counseling is deficient they must enhance it. Recent research has documented that in therapy gifted black students may express the belief that their problems are unique and different from those of other students (Ford, Harris, and Schuerger, 1993). According to those authors, it is important for gifted students to establish "universality," whereby they understand that they are not so different from other students. Forming these connections to other students is important because gifted black students who see themselves as having a "unique" set of problems often have feelings of isolation and stress. Counselors who work with gifted black students can play a very critical role in helping them sort out their feelings about their identification as gifted and can help instill hope by connecting gifted students to role models who share similar attributes and abilities.

Factors Affecting the Retention of Black Men

At first glance, it may seem odd to have a segment on retention in a chapter on gifted black men. Gifted students in general are assumed to have minimal academic problems. However, a closer examination reveals that these students have a number of challenges and concerns that can impair their academic progress. Whereas gifted students are assumed to have minimal difficulty, black male students are assumed to have considerable difficulty. Hence, duality and conflict are often experienced by gifted black men. No matter how academically capable a student is, the collegiate experience can present a number of obstacles that can impede academic progress. Finally, this segment is important because of the noticeable decline in black men on college campuses. Mow and Nettles (1990) report that although minority groups in general have made progress over the past decade, blacks have not. They report that "for blacks, overall enrollment declined, and the decline was particularly sharp among black males" (p. 45). More recently, the *Fourteenth Annual Status Report of Minorities in Higher Education* indicates that African American college enrollment has increased by 16.1 percent since 1990 (American Council on Education, 1995–96); yet despite this improvement, blacks continue to fall below the improvements of Asians, Hispanics, and American Indians. These trends illustrate how critical it is for educators to support and understand the problems of black men who are enrolled in higher education.

Unlike the status of research on the gifted and talented, the retention literature has explored the factors surrounding the academic and social experiences of black students in greater depth. Specific studies on gifted black students and retention are rare. However, a number of studies of retention have examined issues for black men separate from other groups. A number of themes are well documented in the retention literature: (1) the high attrition rate of black men in college, (2) the fact that students with financial aid are more likely to matriculate and graduate, (3) the likelihood that black students who enter college with strong academic preparation and have access to academic support services will persist and graduate, and (4) the impeding effect on black students of racial hostility on predominantly white campuses.

For black men in particular, two additional elements are worth exploring in greater detail: their interactions with faculty, and institutional and environmental factors.

Interactions with Faculty. The academic experiences that students have are important to their overall success. A primary link to the academic life of a campus often begins with interactions with faculty. Research has found that the role of faculty, particularly outside the classroom, is important in retaining students (Pascarella and Terenzini, 1979). For black male students, these relationships can be difficult to establish. Jacqueline Fleming's extensive study, *Blacks in College* (1984), reveals that senior black men on predominantly white campuses expressed concern about their relationships with faculty and administrators. According to Fleming, "their specific complaint about teachers is that they do not grade fairly" (p. 73). These black men in Fleming's study had higher scores than their black female counterparts on academic stress indicators such as personal life and a sense of personal threat. Fleming notes that "One of the most discouraging aspects of male development is that senior males report being less energetic than freshmen. The academic demotivation that is apparent among these males certainly suggests that energy is withdrawn from academics" (1984, p. 73). Allen (1992) reports that those students who displayed higher levels of self-confidence and higher levels of aspirations were more likely to report favorable relationships with faculty (p. 35). Similarly, Fries-Britt (1994) concludes that for a small select population of gifted black collegians at a predominantly white campus, their relationships with the faculty were very positive. In part, these strong relations may be due to the academic capabilities of the students and the high-profile program in which the students were enrolled.

Institutional and Environmental Factors. Research on academic achievement of black students indicates that black students who attend historically black colleges report higher levels of academic achievement than blacks enrolled at predominantly white colleges (Fleming, 1984; Allen, 1992). Black students on predominantly white campuses report feelings of academic and social isolation, alienation, and racial discrimination. At historically black institutions, they report feeling connection to the campus, acceptance, and encouragement to succeed.

Research indicates that black men are more adversely affected by inter-racial environments. Fleming (1984) identifies a combination of factors that contribute to the sense of deterioration black men experience: loss in intel-lectual gains, interpersonal hostility, and a shifting of "turf" on a white cam-pus that results in loss of the male dominance they enjoy on black campuses. Allen (1992) concludes that black men attending predominantly white schools report lower levels of self-confidence as compared to black women. The research of Mow and Nettles (1990) indicates that blacks and whites have different perceptions about the quality of college life for minorities: "some 92 percent of black students and 96 percent of black faculty and staff cited feelings of alienation and loneliness as reasons for minority attrition, while 74 percent of white faculty and administrators had that perception" (p. 79). University faculty and staff must recognize that minorities' perceptions about the campus environment are important. Subtle as well as blatant messages that are communicated to black students by what is valued and practiced in the campus environment, traditions, and customs can serve as barriers to their success.

Implementing Successful Intervention Programs

The challenges and issues faced by gifted black collegians certainly suggest how important are support programs providing academic enhancement, con-nections to other gifted students, and opportunities to explore career endeav-ors. Although many colleges and universities have honors programs, they may not be attractive to gifted black students. Gifted minority students may shy away from honors programs, especially on predominantly white campuses, because of the stereotyped perceptions that others often have about blacks' being less intelligent (Harvey, 1986) and blacks' perceptions of these programs as activities that whites—or those acting white—engage in.

At the same time, the increase in honors programs in historically black institutions suggests that racial and ethnic minority students "can feel comfort-able in displaying their talents to their full potential and free to enjoy the rewards of the aggressiveness and hard work without the fear of being treated as outcasts by a white majority who might resent their academic success" (p. 45). The reluctance of blacks to participate, even if by choice, should not serve as an excuse for program staff to avoid recruiting and pursuing these stu-dents (Harvey, 1986). Honors programs especially on white campuses should strive to create a "critical mass" of gifted black students even if they show reluc-tance to participate. Given the negative experience of black men on white cam-puses, combined with the low enrollment and retention rates for those students, colleges and universities must create opportunities especially for black men to connect. Creating a critical mass provides these students a level of support that has been found to be important (Fries-Britt, 1994). For some students, a critical mass of other gifted blacks creates the "like type" community they find helpful and supportive as they integrate academically and socially into the larger campus milieu (Fries-Britt, 1994). Research indicates that gifted black students tend to express more of a need for such special programs and services as study skills, personal counseling, independent study, honors courses, financial aid, and employment (Kerr, Colangelo, Maxey, and Christensen, 1992).

The Meyerhoff Scholars Program

One program designed to address these and other needs has made a million-dollar commitment to gifted blacks and other gifted populations. The Meyerhoff Scholars Program at the University of Maryland, Baltimore County, originally was established to increase the number of blacks, especially black men, in science and engineering. The first all-male class of Meyerhoff Scholars enrolled in fall 1989. Subsequent classes began to enroll black women, who were equally underserved. In 1996 the program expanded to include members of other groups. However, the program majority remains male and overwhelmingly African American, with a central focus on the issues of African Americans, in particular men.

The program is based on a philosophy that all of the African American students selected can succeed in science and engineering as long as the necessary resources and opportunities for support are available. The success of the Meyerhoff Program can be attributed to the extensive network of support the program receives, starting with the Robert and Jane Meyerhoff Foundation and the exceptional commitment of the president of the university, Freeman Hrabowski, who established the program during his years as provost on the campus.

The Meyerhoff Program employs a number of interventions and resources to help these gifted students succeed, beginning with initial contact and recruitment.

Recruitment. With the help of high school personnel, university administrators identify top math and science students to recruit to the program in their senior year. The selection process includes an on-campus weekend visit, where the students and their parents have an opportunity to meet university officials, Meyerhoff students, and their parents.

Summer Bridge Program. During the summer preceding enrollment, the students attend a six-week, on-campus program where they have an opportunity to take several classes. They receive credit for a math course and an African American studies course; they also take two noncredit courses, one in chemistry and physics and the other in study skills. The students have an opportunity to review some of the material covered in high school and to become familiar with the material they will learn in college. In addition to the academic aspect of the summer program, students participate in social, cultural, and recreational activities.

Scholarship Support. The Meyerhoff students receive significant financial support. The full scholars receive a four-year comprehensive scholarship, while finalists receive more limited financial support. Students must maintain a B average and remain enrolled in mathematics, science, or engineering.

Study Groups. Studying in groups is highly encouraged because program staff believe that group study leads to content mastery, peer support, role modeling, motivation, and a sense of group belonging.

Program Values. The Meyerhoff Program was developed with a set of core values that are emphasized throughout the program: seeking help with tutoring and advisement counseling; striving for outstanding academic achievement; serving as a support for fellow Meyerhoffs; getting involved in research; interacting with faculty; participating in class; working with other high performers (including students of different ethnic and cultural backgrounds); preparing for graduate study; and establishing a sense of commitment to contribute to the African American and broader community after graduation.

Program Community. Strong emphasis is placed on the community created by the Meyerhoff Program. The program serves as a campus-based support system and community for students. Regular meetings are held with the students and staff to discuss a wide range of issues, including academic achievement and personal concerns. These meetings also are used to strengthen and reinforce high expectations, peer support, and solidarity.

Personal Advising and Counseling. The program is administered by professional staff who provide personal advising and counseling for the students. The staff consists of a full-time academic adviser, an executive director, a director, and an assistant director. Together, these individuals provide direction and support for the students.

Tutoring. The students are encouraged to participate in the tutorial services that are offered by the several departments. If additional tutoring is required, the program staff works with departments to provide it.

Summer Research Internships. Tremendous efforts are made to provide summer internships with professionals in the field in order to strengthen students' work habits, enhance their research skills, increase their interest in their field, and establish future contacts for graduate study and, ultimately, work opportunities.

Faculty Involvement. Department chairs and faculty participate in recruitment activities, research mentorship, teaching, and special events. The program staff and faculty work together to discuss the demands of the courses and identify how to enhance student performance.

Administrative Involvement and Public Support. The Meyerhoff Program receives significant support from the campus leadership. The president's office, executive vice president, deans, department chairs, and program directors contribute to the success of the program. Moreover, there is substantial public support. From the governor's office to community leaders, the Meyerhoff Program is highly visible and supported.

Mentors. Mentors for the Meyerhoffs are recruited from top professionals in the field. Many of these individuals serve as role models, support, and "advisers" to the Meyerhoff scholars.

Family Involvement. The family members of the Meyerhoffs are invited, whenever possible, to participate in special activities and meetings. Parents are informed of students' problems and invited to problem-solving meetings. An association has been formed by the parents to serve as a resource for students, parents, and program staff.

The thirteen components of the program work together to form a foundation to address four primary areas: (1) skills and knowledge, (2) motivation and support, (3) academic and social integration, and (4) monitoring and advising. The Meyerhoff Program has been extremely successful and is able to report significant outcomes and accomplishments. The program reports a retention rate of 96.5 percent. Students have selected majors in broadly distributed scientific and technical fields: biological sciences, biochemistry, computer science, mechanical engineering, mathematics, chemical engineering, engineering science, interdisciplinary studies, chemistry, and physics. Many of the Meyerhoff students have completed research internships with nationally and internationally recognized laboratories throughout the United States and abroad. Summer 1995 placements included MIT's Biotechnology Process Engineering Center, Harvard University Medical School's Hematology/Oncology Department, and the NIH's National Center for Human Genome Research, to identify just a few. Graduates of the program have received fellowships or scholarships to prestigious graduate programs around the country, including Harvard, MIT, Yale, Johns Hopkins, Morehouse, Stanford, Duke, Howard, Princeton, Carnegie Mellon, and Michigan.

The success of students in programs like the Meyerhoff invariably raise the legitimate question of how to determine if the program is making a difference when the population is already talented. There is supportive research that internal sources of motivation often account for the success of black male students. However, evidence also indicates that intervention efforts such as the Meyerhoff Program can enhance academic performance. In a study designed to determine the impact of the program, Fries-Britt (1994) found that the Meyerhoff program contributed to the students' academic success. Students identified the academic enhancements offered by the program, opportunities to work with other bright black students, and positive interactions with faculty and program staff as factors that contributed to their success.

Creating new programs like the Meyerhoff Scholars Program is not always an option, but it should continue to be a goal. In light of limited resources, it is difficult for colleges and universities to create new programs while maintaining existing honors efforts. However, existing programs might be enhanced by employing some of the methods and interventions that have been successful for this population.

Recommendations

- Support and conduct extensive research on gifted black men.
- Look for examples of high achievement and capability in black men who demonstrate a wide range of capabilities, including intelligence, leadership, artistic ability, communication, and so on.
- Recruit and encourage the participation of gifted black men in existing honors programs.
- Establish a support network (critical mass) of gifted black students. If possible, a scholarship or honors program should be established to meet the unique needs of gifted black students.
- Work with faculty to increase their understanding of the needs of all black students, especially the issues experienced by gifted black students.
- Encourage gifted black students to network with a diverse group of students, especially the larger community of black students.
- Help gifted black students make connections with mentors and professionals who share their abilities and interests.

Summary

This chapter has sought to raise awareness of a distinct and often neglected segment of the black student population, gifted black men. It demonstrates that little is known about this population and what influences their college experience. The research that has been conducted clearly points to a need for more extensive studies on this extraordinary community of black students. The increasing public discourse on the status of black men must be expanded to include a comprehensive representation of the multiple communities in which they participate and succeed. Few would argue that there are plenty of negative images of black men, almost to the exclusion of the positive. Black men have not exclusively participated in any one of the activities that they have been associated with, such as drugs, crime, and athletics; rather, they have been drawn upon disproportionately as examples to reinforce racial and social stereotypes. It is time to balance the scales. Examples of positive role models and black male excellence are abundant; what is absent is the commitment to correct the public image. Faculty and administrators can start by changing those attitudes and practices on our own campuses that impede the progress of black men. The set of recommendations herein represents a modest start.

References

Allen, W. R. "The Color of Success: African-American College Student Outcomes at Predominantly White and Historically Black Public Colleges and Universities." *Harvard Educational Review*, 1992, *62* (1), 26–44.

American Council on Education. *Minorities in Higher Education, Fourteenth Annual Status Report*. Washington, D.C.: American Council on Education, 1995–96.

Baldwin, A. Y. "Gifted Black Adolescents: Beyond Racism to Pride." In M. Bireley and J. Genshaft (eds.), *Understanding the Gifted Adolescent: Education, Developmental, and Multicultural Issues.* New York: Teachers College Press, 1991.

Banks, J. A. "The Historical Reconstruction of Knowledge About Race: Implications for Transformative Teaching." *Educational Researcher,* 1995, *24* (2), 15–25.

Chiu, L. H. "Self-Esteem of Gifted, Normal, and Mild Mentally Handicapped Children." *Psychology in the Schools,* 1990, *127,* 263–265.

Colangelo, N. "Counseling Needs of Culturally Diverse Gifted Students." *Roeper Review,* 1985, *8,* 33–35.

Cooley, M. R., Cornell, D. G., and Lee, C. "Peer Acceptance and Self-Concept of Black Students in a Summer Gifted Program." *Journal for the Education of the Gifted,* 1991, *14* (2), 166–177.

Fleming, J. *Blacks in College: A Comparative Study of Students' Success in Black and White Institutions.* San Francisco: Jossey-Bass, 1984.

Ford, D. Y. "Desegregating Gifted Education: A Need Unmet." *Journal of Negro Education,* 1995, *64* (1), 52–62.

Ford, D. Y. *Reversing Underachievement Among Gifted Black Students: Promising Practices and Programs.* Education and Psychology of the Gifted Series. New York: Teachers College Press, Columbia University, 1996.

Ford, D., and Harris, J. "On Discovering the Hidden Treasure of Gifted and Talented Black Children." *Roeper Review,* 1990, *13,* 27–32.

Ford, D. Y., and Harris III, J. "Black Students: 'At Promise' Not 'At Risk' for Giftedness." *Journal of Human Behavior and Learning,* 1991, *7* (2), 21–29.

Ford, D. Y., Harris III, J., and Schuerger, J. "Racial Identity Development Among Gifted Students: Counseling Issues and Concerns." *Journal of Counseling and Development,* 1993, *71,* 409–417.

Fordham, S. "Racelessness as a Strategy in Black Students' School Success: Pragmatic Strategy or Pyrrhic Victory?" *Harvard Educational Review,* 1988, *58* (1), 54–84.

Fordham, S., and Ogbu, J. "Black Students' School Success: Coping with the Burden of 'Acting White.'" *Urban Review,* 1986, *18* (3), 176–207.

Fries-Britt, S. "A Test of Tinto's Retention Theory on the Meyerhoff Scholars: A Case Study Analysis." Unpublished doctoral dissertation, Department of Educational Policy, Planning, and Administration, University of Maryland, 1994.

Gardner, H. *Frames of Mind: The Theory of Multiple Intelligences.* New York: Basic Books, 1983.

George, V. "Talented Adolescent Women and Motive to Avoid Success." *Multicultural Counseling and Development,* 1986, *14,* 132–139.

Hadaway, N., and Marek-Schroer, M. F. "Multidimensional Assessment of the Gifted Minority Students." *Roeper Review,* 1992, *15* (2), 73–77.

Harvey, M.L.A. "Minorities and Women in Honors Education." In P. G. Friedman and R. C. Jenkins-Friedman (eds.), *Fostering Academic Excellence Through Honors Programs.* San Francisco: Jossey-Bass, 1986.

Herrnstein, R. J., and Murray, C. *The Bell Curve.* New York: Free Press, 1994.

Hollingworth, L. S. *Children Above 180 IQ.* New York: World Book, 1942.

Hrabowski III, F. A. "Helping Gifted Black Males Succeed in Science." *Journal of Health Care for the Poor and Underserved,* 1991, *2* (1), 197–201.

Kerr, B. A., and Colangelo, N. "The College Plans of Academically Talented Students." *Journal of Counseling and Development,* 1988, *67,* 42–48.

Kerr, B., Colangelo, N., Maxey, J., and Christensen, P. "Characteristics of Academically Talented Minority Students." *Journal of Counseling and Development,* 1992, *70,* 606–609.

Kitano, M. K. "Testing and Identification: Intellectual Abilities and Psychological Intensities in Young Children: Implications for the Gifted." *Roeper Review,* 1990, *13,* 5–10.

Kitano, M. K. "Lessons from Gifted Women of Color." *Journal of Secondary Gifted Education,* Winter 1994/1995, 176–187.

Lindstrom, R., and Van Sant, S. "Special Issues in Working with Gifted Minority Adolescents." *Counseling and Development,* 1986, *64,* 583–586.

Masten, W. G. "Identification of Gifted Minority Students: Past Research, Future Directions." *Roeper Review,* 1985, *8* (2), 83–85.

Mow, S. L., and Nettles, M. "Minority Student Access to, and Persistence and Performance in, College: A Review of the Trends and Research Literature." In J. C. Smart (ed.), *Higher Education: Handbook of Theory and Research, Vol. VI.* New York: Agathon Press, 1990.

Pascarella, E. T., and Terenzini, P. "Patterns of Student Faculty Informal Interaction Beyond the Classroom and Voluntary Freshman Attendance." *Journal of Higher Education,* 1979, *48,* 540–552.

Piirto, J. *Talented Children and Adults: Their Development and Education.* New York: Macmillan, 1994.

Renzulli, J. S. "The Three-Ring Conception of Giftedness: A Developmental Model for Creative Productivity." In R. J. Sternberg and J. E. Davidson (eds.), *Conceptions of Giftedness.* Cambridge, England: Cambridge University Press, 1986.

Sternberg, R. J., and Davidson, J. E. *Conceptions of Giftedness.* Cambridge, England: Cambridge University Press, 1986.

Terman, L. *Genetic Studies of Genius.* Vol. 1: *Mental and Physical Traits of a Thousand Gifted Children.* Stanford, Calif.: Stanford University Press, 1925.

Yong, F. L. "Self-Concepts, Locus of Control, and Machiavellianism of Ethnically Diverse Middle School Students Who Are Gifted." *Roeper Review,* 1994, *16* (3), 192–194.

SHARON FRIES-BRITT is an assistant professor in higher education at the University of Maryland, College Park. Prior to her academic appointment, she worked in student affairs administration.

Approximately one out of nine African American male college students is an athlete. For this reason, studies that focus on successful retention and graduation of this population can have a significant impact on the overall success of black male undergraduates.

Retention Issues and Models for African American Male Athletes

Dawn R. Person, Kenya M. LeNoir

Historically, this society has viewed securing a higher education degree as a major link to social class status and attainment of wealth. African American students as a whole constitute only 8.7 percent of college enrollments and a very low 5.7 percent of college graduates (Justiz, Wilson, and Bjork, 1994). Given the attrition rate of this population on college campuses, the need to look at possible strategies that will increase retention is paramount. In presenting undergraduate enrollment data for all students, the National Collegiate Athletic Association (NCAA) reports that at Division I schools 45 percent more African American women are enrolled than are African American men (158,095 women to 108,606 men), but in terms of student athletes there are 3.2 times as many African American male athletes as African American female athletes (12,195 men versus 3,591 women) and those black male athletes make up nearly one-third of the total number of all male student athletes (39,561). These numbers reveal that about one out of every nine African American male students at predominantly white four-year institutions is an athlete.

The graduation rate for the entering class of 1990 after six years was 40 percent for African American male students not involved in athletics (*NCAA Division I Graduation Rates Report*, 1996). Conversely, graduation rates in revenue-generating sports for African American male student athletes at predominantly white campuses were 37 percent in baseball, 38 percent in basketball, 43 percent in track and field, and 43 percent in football (*NCAA Division I Graduation Rates Report*, 1996). Accordingly, African American male student athletes graduate at a slightly higher rate than African American male nonathletes. However, the issue is not whether the black athletes fare better than the black nonathletes; rather, it is that both populations graduated at a rate less than that of student athletes in general.

Clearly, steps need to be taken to uncover what solutions can effectively help African American male student athletes (as well as all other African American students) persist toward degree completion. This chapter specifically addresses the issues that face these students on our campuses. We start by providing a review of the demographic and psychosocial background of this specific population in higher education in an effort to place the issue within a context. Secondly, we give an overview of the literature on retention in student affairs, which shows correlational experiences to be used when working with this population of students. Lastly, we describe strategies and initiatives, and practical recommendations based on a research study, so that the reader is better equipped to respond to the needs of African American male student athletes.

Demographics

African American male student athletes are as diverse as any other student culture on campus; however, trends have been identified specific to this population. In 1987, the NCAA produced the findings from a research study conducted by the American Institute for Research entitled "The Experiences of Black Intercollegiate Athletes at NCAA Division I Institutions" (Center for the Study of Athletics, 1987). It revealed that nearly one-half of all black football players and basketball players came from the lowest socioeconomic quartile, where the mean family income is $17,500 per year. These athletes were most likely from women-headed households where the eleventh grade was the median level of parental education and most parental occupations were given as unskilled labor or clerical. These data reflect a high first-generation college student population.

Academically, the study also showed that nearly 60 percent of blacks scored in the lowest quartile of both the SAT and ACT, while 6 percent scored in the highest quartile. Black male athletes in the study made up 48 percent of the lowest quartile for high school grades and 61 percent of the lowest quartile for college grade point average, with the mean being 2.16. Because athletes spend so much of their time with athletic-related activities, they tend to spend less time with other endeavors. The study showed that on average black male athletes spent twenty-eight hours preparing for and participating in their sport and twenty-three hours preparing for class; on average they missed two classes per week during the season and one class during the off-season. Edwards (1990) reminds us that some student athletes spend upwards of forty hours a week on their sport, and when they are done practicing or playing they are often in pain from the intense physical activity or suffering from a combination of mental, physical, and emotional exhaustion; as a consequence, the motivation to study loses priority to getting rest. The majority of black male athletes do not major in physical education, as is often assumed; rather, the largest number report a major in business administration. The survey reveals that although black male athletes place high priority on completing their degrees, education is not their primary goal, and it reveals that had they not been recruited for athletics many would not be attending college.

Challenges for the African American Male Student Athlete

African American male student athletes specifically have to negotiate the dualism of being students and athletes, not to mention the other roles they fulfill; this causes them to experience a range of emotions based on precollege and college experiences. These include both the positive and negative stereotypes and expectations that one associates with student athletes and black men.

Academic and social integration can be difficult for most first-time college students; the added responsibility student athletes face upon entering college can oftentimes be overwhelming. Highly solicited scholarship athletes are courted by the university and placed on a pedestal. But when the athlete arrives on campus, he becomes just another athlete who has to adjust to a period of derecruitment by transitioning away from the attention of coaches as the season for soliciting new recruits begins. This loss of individual attention, along with the shock many student athletes feel when they arrive on campus as the high school superstar only to find many of their professors, administrators, and peers view them as no more than a "dumb jock," can further lead to their feelings of deflated self-esteem, abandonment, and isolation (Funk, 1991). Lapchick (1987) states that frequently the black male athlete's sense of responsibility has been diminished by parents, coaches, and the media, and in that process his sense of self-worth off the field is virtually nonexistent. A UCLA study found that black families are four times as likely to view their children's involvement in athletics as something that may lead to a professional sports career (Funk, 1991). Edwards (1990) states that the myths and stereotypes created by the media and the student's home experiences are often further supported by the educational system, thereby creating in children a false sense of the reality of a possible career in professional sport.

Discussing the stereotypes surrounding blacks in sports, Harris (1989) credits these myths either to overemphasis on sport by black youth, which has been detrimental to the black community, or to the proponents who see the accomplishments of professional athletes as a boost for the black community. He studied black and white youths at a summer camp and arrived at several conclusions. Blacks are more likely than whites to perceive themselves as being good at sports. Blacks are economically poorer than whites, yet they still aspire to attend college. Harris suggests that perhaps blacks are using athletics as a method of bridging the gap to the mainstream and to being successful. Underwood (1984) shows that in a five-year study of five hundred Michigan State University student athletes 62 percent were encouraged by their fathers at an early age to participate in athletics, and in most cases researchers suggest that adults emphasize sports to children as a means of engaging them in the American values system. If sports are a method by which American values and beliefs are transferred en route to the American dream, issues of race and class have also been added stressors to the life of the African American male athlete.

The realities of race and class for many student athletes further their sense of disillusionment and isolation on campus. Smedley, Meyers, and Harrell (1993) regard experiences of racism and discrimination on campus as a psychological and sociocultural stressor that could lead to the maladjustment of minority students. Tracey and Sedlacek (1985), Fleming (1984), and Astin (1993) all regard racist experiences in college as one of the main variables explaining differences in academic performance, social and psychological adjustment, and levels of involvement between minorities and nonminorities on college campuses.

Black men arrive on campus having to deal with others' perceptions of them and the myths and stereotypes associated with them. Dealy (1990) states that in particular black male athletes on white campuses experience depression often related to direct incidents of racism and discrimination; frequently, they do not feel entirely welcome on campus, but instead as if their only purpose is to win football and basketball games. Schlossberg, Lynch, and Chickering (1989) discuss the idea of students' being in a state of marginality upon entering and during their years in college. The authors conclude that the more we can get the student to feel he or she matters (that is, commands the attention of others, feels important and appreciated, and believes that others need him or her too as a vital part of the community), the more involved and attached he or she becomes to the institution. The more attached and involved the student feels to the institution, the more likely he or she is to persist.

Positive Attributes for the African American Male Student Athlete

On the other end of the spectrum, there are some advantages for African American male student athletes. Farrell (1996) states that the climate of the campus is more conducive to African American athletes than to the general African American student community. They have athletics-related aid, and those who are doing well in sports have the motivation to continue without stopping along the way. Student athletes are oftentimes highly involved in their college careers. Astin (1985) states that involvement denotes physical and psychological energy given to academics; in 1987, he broadened the concept to include athletics, noting that athletics parallels academics. Student athletes often are committed to the institution on all levels. Given the importance placed on college students' mattering, the notions of involvement and persistence, along with the unique characteristics and psychosocial factors that affect African American male student athletes, the literature on retention is central to understanding effective initiatives for the persistence of African American male student athletes.

Retention

There is little research conducted on why some African American male athletes persist toward degree completion and others do not. The literature of retention in higher education, however, does show that increased support can enhance students' experiences on campus. Therefore, we now explore retention theories in higher education and how they can be translated into developing specific interventions to be used with African American male student athletes and African American male students in general.

Theories and Theoretical Models. Noel, Levitz, Saluri, and Associates (1985) suggest that there needs to be more effort toward retaining students and demonstrating the importance of institutional commitment from the top down as a method of enhancing students' experiences on campus. Other theorists provide examples of programmatic and policy influences on retention. Tinto (1993) suggests that understanding why students leave is instrumental in designing a retention plan. Students drop out, stop out, or transfer for a number of reasons, some of which are voluntary or personal while others are involuntary (such as academic dismissal); all are due to some incongruence between the individual and the system.

Tinto believes that individual departure results from interactions between the student and the educational environment over time. The key element of Tinto's theory is that the student's interaction with the educational environment directly affects how and whether the student integrates into the educational environment and whether the integration is paramount to the student's persistence. To ensure that students are incorporated into their new environment, Tinto suggests that colleges implement effective retention plans.

Essential elements of an effective retention plan include assessment, planning, implementation, evaluation, and reformation. More importantly, top-level administrative commitment and institutional commitment are paramount (Tinto, 1993). Forrest (1985) states that a group of nine institutions with the most comprehensive orientation and advising programs have a graduation rate 9 percent higher than the group of nine institutions having the least comprehensive orientation and advising plans. Although general retention strategies are somewhat effective, specialized approaches to support African American male students and student athletes warrant further exploration.

Carr (1992) examined fourth-semester persistence rates of black male athletes and investigated the effects of athletic and academic support programs on persistence. The study showed that 100 percent of the black male athletes involved in a highly supported basketball program persisted for four semesters. Significant components of Carr's highly supported basketball program were an orientation, communication between instructors and coaches, ongoing academic progress review, and tutoring for the student in the "home turf" or athletic department. Both Forrest's and Carr's studies demonstrate that implementing added and comprehensive support—such as early intervention, extensive orientation, and advising programs—can benefit students and aid their overall retention.

Strategies and Initiatives. Other initiatives that have proven to be successful in retaining African American men, particularly athletes, are in the area of mentoring. Also, Taylor (1996) reports that attentive instruction, high expectations, and collaborative study have proven beneficial to students and led more of them to completing their degrees. Steele (in Taylor, 1996) believes that one of the keys to successfully retaining students is convincing them that their instructors are allies.

Roper and McKenzie (1987) developed a comprehensive academic advising model for black student athletes, adapted from Douglas Heath's (1977) theoretical model of maturity. A sample of the initiatives suggested by those authors in their comprehensive model includes ongoing assessment for all four undergraduate years, with goal setting and collaborative decision making in year one; group discussions, career counseling, and career discussion in year two; community service, independent study, and public speaking in year three; and updating of goals, leading of discussions, internships, and living transition programs for year four.

The University of Texas at Austin has seen increasing success in retaining their African American male student athletes involved in the Gateway Program by instituting a better tracking system, identifying their students' needs early, and adding more academic advisers. There is also a life skills program called Challenging Athletes' Minds for Personal Success (CHAMPS), designed to address the specific needs of the student athlete academically, personally, and socially, which is being used by many institutions.

One initiative institutions can take in improving this area is to hire more staff of color to serve as role models. The lack of representation in the main offices and coaching staffs mirrors the minimal numbers of African American faculty and staff at institutions; this often leaves the student with very few mentors and adds to their feelings of marginality.

A Research Study

For the past five years, a persistence and evaluation study of 2,395 African American mathematics, science, and engineering students was conducted at seventeen different institutions, all east of the Mississippi. These include both two-year and four-year institutions, predominantly white and historically black, ranging from open admissions to highly selective admission, all committed to developing program and service units to support retention of African American and Hispanic students in mathematics, the sciences, and engineering disciplines. From this study, data were analyzed on thirty-one African American male student athletes from eleven of the seventeen institutions to examine the experience of these students and their persistence and retention in higher education. The institutions range from large conference schools to regional-conference-level athletic programs. For the purposes of this writing, the type of institution and conference level of play is less central than those experiences the African American male student athlete reported as related to his academic and personal development.

Methodology. Annually, random samples of students, faculty, and administrators were surveyed, interviewed, and invited to participate in focus groups at each institution. Responses were elicited to questions concerning the background characteristics of students, experiences at the college, usage and effectiveness of program services, and students' future goals and aspirations. Additionally, multiple site visits to each institution allowed observation of the students' interactions with others and with program services, as well as a sense of the campus climate. Data were analyzed by and across institutions to measure student usage of program services and infer program effectiveness.

Generally, the earlier students enroll in a retention program at one of these institutions, the more likely they are to persist at the institution and in their major. This finding speaks to the need for effective and comprehensive program services for student retention. Those students who persist have parents with college degrees, receive private scholarships at a higher rate, and are less likely to be employed at the school but are much more likely to be involved with research and internship experiences. Most of the persisters are satisfied with their department, set goals for their academic achievement, and expect excellence in their work; twice as many persisters as nonpersisters participate in study groups. Persisters are usually comfortable in their classes, and about one-half are comfortable with administrators and staff. Most feel encouraged by faculty, but more nonpersisters than persisters feel dissatisfied with the guidance and support for future planning that they receive from faculty.

Results. Thirty-one African American male student athletes from eleven institutions participated in this study and were tracked as part of the random selection of students surveyed over time. These institutions are both public (50 percent) and private (50 percent), large (58 percent) and small (42 percent), historically black (21 percent) and predominantly white (79 percent), two-year (16 percent) and four-year (84 percent). Sixty-one percent of the student athletes attend public institutions in this study, while 39 percent are enrolled in private institutions. Almost all of the students indicate that athletic scholarship support was important among their reasons for choosing the institution attended. Financial aid in all forms served as the most important reason for 61 percent of the students.

Many of these students report that their parents had attended college, and some have parents with professional and graduate degrees. Yet, 45 percent of the students are first-generation college students. Thirty-nine percent have mothers with college degrees, and 42 percent of the students' fathers graduated from college. Twenty-nine percent of these students report that both parents were college educated. Only 10 percent of the students report annual family incomes below $15,000, yet almost all are receiving some form of financial aid or scholarship. Approximately 26 percent of these student athletes report working while in school.

Although these students are somewhat reflective of the profile of African American male student athletes described earlier in this chapter, there are some exceptions. Fewer of these students are first-generation college students (50 percent), and fewer are in the lower socioeconomic range. However, similar to the previous study, "The Experiences of Black Intercollegiate Athletes at NCAA Division I Institutions" (Center for the Study of Athletics, 1987), most of these athletes receive financial aid or an athletic scholarship and almost 50 percent were first generation college students. Although there are some differences in the profiles of these students, the first-generation variable, need for financial support, and responsibility to both an athletic program and academic requirements may provide findings and recommendations useful for programs and services for African American student athletes in the future.

Most (68 percent) of the student athletes studied would recommend their institution to other black and Hispanic students. The African American student athlete retention rate is 48 percent. Many factors contribute to this retention rate, such as financial needs being met and the effectiveness of program services offered. More important, however, is the students' regular usage of those program services. Sixty-five percent of these students participate in a summer program, mostly a precollege experience. Tutoring services are used by 68 percent of the students, and 48 percent take advantage of mentoring activities and mentors (peer, alumni, and faculty). About one-half of the students are involved in peer counseling, and 68 percent report participating in study groups for academic support. Almost all students actively engage in advising and advising programs (71 percent), yet less than one-half (45 percent) take advantage of field trip activities. More than one-third of the student athletes are able to engage in research activities and internships even though they had to commit a significant amount of time to a sport. Forty-two percent report having an internship at some point in their studies, and again 45 percent participate in career seminar activities. Overall, these students report high levels of satisfaction with program services across institutions. Some services do receive higher rankings in terms of student satisfaction: summer programs, tutoring for first-year and second-year classes, and research and internship experiences.

In general, these student athletes are more likely to be retained in their degree program if they are involved in a summer program and work in study groups. They are also more inclined to persist when advising, research experiences, and career seminars are viewed as effective. Faculty-student interaction is found to be less frequent outside of the classroom and office hours. At the historically black institutions, there is more interaction between faculty and students, which leads to more student involvement with research and internship programs. Additionally, positive levels of student satisfaction are often attributed by the students to the faculty. Overall, nonpersisters in this study are less likely to engage in research activities; less likely to participate in study groups; and less comfortable with faculty, in classes, and with staff and administrators.

Three Models

As was discussed previously in this chapter, retention programs for African American student athletes should be comprehensive and consider issues from admissions and orientation through graduation. Many different components could be considered for a retention program, but through this study three models emerge as being effective within the institutions studied. The first model is coordinated by a program administrator who is either full-time faculty or in student affairs and provides only focused academic-year support services for students: personal counseling incorporating career and survival skills, tutorials, group study, support for cocurricular activities related to professional development and faculty mentoring, and others.

The second model is coordinated by a faculty member who is advised by a board consisting of faculty and administrators. Students are expected to meet certain criteria to be participants in the program, thus setting the stage for high expectations and high performance on the part of the students. Services provided include academic-year support services, summer research and internship programs, and graduate-school preparation and career-development activities offered to students at each class level.

The third model includes a program director responsible for administering a precollege summer program, academic-year support services, and career-development and graduate-preparation activities. Most of the institutions in this study are represented in the third model described. It brings the student into the academic community before he is indoctrinated into the athletic culture and allows him to spend a concentrated period of time on his academic studies prior to the beginning of the academic year. Most of these programs have a six-to-eight-week summer residential program, where students live and work together with faculty and peer advisers and tutors to hone their study habits, review materials from high school, and preview the first semester of the academic college experience. In most cases, students earn some credit toward their degree in mathematics, English, communications, or a seminar on human development.

During the academic year, students are tracked and academic progress monitored closely so as to identify and resolve problems that arise while they are still surmountable. Throughout the year, students are expected to study in groups, use tutors regularly, seek advice and counsel from staff specially trained to respond to the needs of new students and students of color, and employ the study habits they gained in the summer. Classes may be offered in clusters that allow students to take courses with their summer cohort. Additionally, some classes are offered in extended time periods such that a course in calculus, for example, that would normally meet four times a week meets for five sessions weekly.

The other major component of this model is early involvement of students with career-development and career-exploration activities. Alumni, role models from various disciplines, mentors, and faculty are involved in assisting students in maintaining a strong sense of identity with their chosen major and future profession and developing an understanding of the possible options available to them after graduation, such as entering graduate school, beginning work in their career, and becoming involved in professional development activities. Students visit graduate schools, attend professional meetings with faculty, and are encouraged to be as involved as possible with preprofessional organizations.

African American student athletes are expected to accomplish and achieve at the same level as other students. They attend and participate in the summer program activities and tutorials offered through these retention efforts, and they cooperate with monitoring of progress and academic advising offered through these services. When difficulties occur, students consult with the program staff, faculty mentors, alumni mentors, and their athletic advisers and coaches, who usually work cooperatively to assist the student. This approach affords the student athlete the opportunity to work with both systems (athletic and academic) for support and to be closely aligned with staff, peers, and a community of scholars to assist them in maintaining balance between academic and athletic involvement.

Through these retention program models, almost all of these student athletes persisted through this five-year study. These programs demonstrate that African American male student athletes can be retained with the proper support systems in place, including demonstrated institutional commitment reflected in program services, caring faculty, and campus climates conducive to development of the African American male student athlete.

Recommendations

When considering effective retention programs for African American male student athletes, we are encouraged by the success rates identified in this study. In fact, the eleven institutions combined have a graduation rate that surpasses that of the NCAA. The principles found in the recommendations addressing the needs of African American male student athletes can apply to retention efforts for African American male college students in general. The athletes are but a subset of this population, and opportunities for broader implications for all African American men will be identified. Therefore, effective strategies that generally support black male student retention can be drawn from these suggestions.

Institutional commitment is critical at all levels. Financial support for students, programs, and technology make a difference. Program support allows for retention programs that provide services spanning the entire college experience. Like financial aid and scholarships, which are front-loaded, retention programs that do not begin with a precollege experience and continue through graduation will be found lacking for this population of students.

The models presented in this chapter suggest that structure is important, as are the location and visibility of services and programs. Retention programs must be intentional in design and well thought out in terms of program components, and programmatic issues must be institutionally based. The needs of

the African American student athlete should be at the center of this effort. Genuine partnerships between academic affairs, student affairs, and athletic affairs must occur in an effort to serve students from a holistic perspective. The leadership for these programs should evolve from academic affairs in partnership with student affairs and the support of the athletic staff. Institutional support for African American male student athletes must consider all aspects of the student and his development, including the family, finances, cultural identity development, self-esteem and self-worth off the playing field, and role models for academic and athletic purposes. Monitoring of student progress is essential and should be part of the institutional research office so that trends and issues in student recruitment, retention, persistence, and graduation can be studied and understood by race, gender, and academic class status.

Retention programs should introduce the student athlete to the academic culture of the college, with all the expectations that will be required of him for success, *before* he is challenged by the rigors of the athletic program and introduced to the student athlete culture. All expectations should be clearly defined and spelled out with the student, and he should be held to the highest of standards within his ability range both in the classroom and on the court or field. It should behoove each institution to consider the climate that African American male students are invited to join, and to ensure their self-worth and dignity in the classrooms, residential halls, and athletic programs. This requires a marked level of sensitivity to race and cultural issues for all involved.

Assessment and evaluation must be systematic and ongoing. Both internal and external experts should be involved in this process and should consider the contextual and institutional factors that affect student retention.

Recruitment and retention of African American faculty, coaches, and other athletic staff; student affairs staff; and other administrators is the key to retaining these students. Students' feelings and levels of satisfaction with the institution are tied to interactions with faculty and others as role models.

Career seminars and research activities support retention of black male athletes, as is true for all African American men; such career development efforts should be an integral part of any retention effort. Another factor that contributes to the climate of the campus is having a critical mass of African American student athletes and African American student nonathletes who can provide peer support so as to positively affect student success. Summer programs that include academic, cultural, career-development, and service-learning or community-service components are viewed as effective by these student athletes.

Summary

Retention researchers stress the importance of integrating students into the college system as necessary. Models of retention are only as good as their ability to function within the institutional culture. Caring faculty, quality teaching, financial aid support, resources for services (such as making staff available), and student involvement in campus life are but some of the factors cited repeatedly in the literature. Student athletes of color, like their nonathlete counterparts, must feel comfortable within the community. Researchers find that grade performance is influenced by students' level of comfort and satisfaction with the environment.

The literature surrounding the African American man on college campuses is complex, in that within the population there are a wide variety of needs to be met. Here we have discussed one subset of the overall population, the African American male student athlete. While these athletes graduate at a slightly higher rate than African American male students who are nonathletes, within the revenue-generating sports such as basketball and football the numbers are still low at 38 percent and 43 percent, respectively, and they show that not even one-half of that population complete their degrees within six years. Realizing that students enter colleges and universities with different educational socialization, as educators we should investigate to see what initiatives can be implemented in aiding students to become successful and complete their degrees.

Institutional accountability and responsibility suggest that universities (faculty, administration, and students) and organizations (for example the NCAA, the Urban League, or the National Science Foundation) should collaborate to provide outreach and support aimed at meeting the needs of the African American male student athlete as well as other African American male students. This population of students in turn will be charged with the responsibility of complementing institutional initiatives by persisting and eventually completing their degrees. With these initiatives and efforts, we can only expect that more progress will be made in the next century.

References

Astin, A. W. *What Matters in College: Four Critical Years Revisited.* San Francisco: Jossey-Bass, 1993.

Carr, P. "College Success and the Black Male." Research report no. 138. San Jose State University, San Jose, Calif.: Evergreen Community College District, 1992.

Center for the Study of Athletics. "The Experiences of Black Intercollegiate Athletes at NCAA Division I Institutions." Studies of Intercollegiate Athletics, no. 3. Washington, D.C.: American Institute for Research, 1987.

Dealy, F. X. *Win at Any Cost.* New York: Birch Lane Press, Carol Publishing Group, 1990.

Edwards, H. In M. Sperber (ed.), *College Sports Inc.* New York: Henry Holt, 1990.

Farrell, C. "Is the NCAA Playing a Numbers Game?" *Black Issues in Higher Education,* 1996, 13 (14), 16–18.

Fleming, J. *Blacks in College: A Comparative Study of Students' Success in Black and White Institutions.* San Francisco: Jossey-Bass, 1984.

Forrest, A. *Creating Conditions for Student and Institutional Success.* In D. Noel, R. Levitz, D. Saluri, and Associates (eds.), *Increasing Student Retention: Effective Programs and Practices for Reducing the Drop-out Rate.* San Francisco: Jossey-Bass, 1985.

Funk, G. *Major Violation: The Unbalanced Priorities in Athletics and Academics.* Champaign, Ill.: Leisure Press, 1991.

Harris, O. "Sport and Race: A Comparison of the Social and Academic Worlds of Black and White Student Athletes (Social World, Academic World)." Dissertation Abstracts International, 50-07A, 1989. (No. 892444161 University of Maryland at College Park)

Hayes, D. W. "Balancing the Ball." Black Issues in Higher Education, 1995, 12 (3), 24–26.

Heath, D. Maturity and Competence: A Transcultural View. New York: Gardners Press, 1997.

Justiz, M. J., Wilson, W., and Bjork, L. G. Minorities in Higher Education. Phoenix, Ariz.: American Council on Education and Oryx Press, 1944.

Lapchick, R. On the Mark. San Francisco: New Lexington Press, 1987.

Lapchick, R. E. "Academic Standards for Athletics in Black and White." Black Issues in Higher Education, 1995, 12, 48–50.

Lapchick, R. E., and Slaughter, J. B. The Rules of the Game: Ethics in College Sport. New York: American Council on Education, Macmillan, 1989.

NCAA Division I Graduation Rates Reports. Overland Park, Kans.: National Collegiate Athletic Association, 1996.

Noel, L., Levitz, R., Saluri, D., and Associates (eds.). Increasing Student Retention: Effective Programs and Practices for Reducing the Drop-out Rate. San Francisco: Jossey-Bass, 1985.

Roper, L. D., and McKenzie, A. "Academic Advising: A Developmental Model for Black Student-Athletes." NASPA Journal, 1987, 26 (2), 91–98.

Schlossberg, N. K., Lynch, A. Q., and Chickering, A. W. Improving Higher Education Environments for Adults: Responsive Programs and Services from Entry to Departure. San Francisco: Jossey-Bass, 1989.

Smedley, B. D., Meyers, H. F., and Harrell, S. P. "Minority Status Stresses and College Adjustment of Ethnic Minority Freshmen." Journal of Higher Education, 1993, 64, 434–452.

Taylor, R. A. "A Degree of Success." Black Issues in Higher Education, 1996, 13 (26), 18–20.

Tinto, V. Leaving College: Rethinking the Causes and Cures of Student Attrition. Second edition. Chicago: University of Chicago Press, 1993.

Tracey, T. J., and Sedlacek, W. E. "The Relationship of Non-Cognitive Variables to Academic Success: A Longitudinal Comparison by Race." Journal of College Student Personnel, 1985, 26, 405–410.

Underwood, C. The Student Athlete. Michigan: Michigan State University Press, 1984.

DAWN R. PERSON is an associate professor in the Department of Organization and Leadership at California State University at Long Beach.

KENYA M. LENOIR is a doctoral student of higher and adult education at Teachers College, Columbia University.

This chapter presents a synopsis of the major conclusions of this volume and a short annotated list of recommended readings for further investigation of the topic.

Conclusions and Recommended Readings

Michael J. Cuyjet

This volume is certainly not intended to be an exhaustive treatment of the myriad issues relating to African American men's experiences on college and university campuses. Many issues that have significant impact on the lives of African American male students on the college campus (for example, black men's socialization patterns, both interracial and self-separationist; black male-female relationships; delivery of student services to black men, especially financial aid; special concerns of black male graduate students; or specific effects of institutionalized racism) have not been addressed here mainly for lack of space. Rather, the material included in this book is a sampling of representative topics by which the authors hope to stimulate interest, discussion, inquiry, and ideas. Even on the particular topics addressed, this material is intended to be more a prototypical illustration than a comprehensive, definitive statement. The editor and the authors hope that the readers will use this material in this spirit and engage in a renewed effort to enhance the college and university experiences of black men.

It is well documented that African American men as a percentage of this country's population are underrepresented in the nation's predominantly white colleges and universities, particularly in relation to the numbers of African American women on the campuses. Many black men encounter significant obstacles in getting admitted to college and continue to face challenges as they matriculate. By reviewing black men's responses to survey questions, we find it apparent that their experiences on campus—at least judging by their perceptions—are somewhat different from those of their white counterparts, or even those of black women.

If black men's college experiences are rather different from those of other students, it would seem reasonable that the theories student affairs practitioners use to understand and focus student development may not apply in the same manner to African American male students. Student affairs administrators may need to gain an understanding of several new theories based on an Africentric philosophy and to learn a new set of application techniques focused on the self-efficacy of the individual student in order to maximize the way in which student service professionals assist African American male students in their personal development.

Positive classroom experiences are critical to successful inclusion of African American men in the campus community. Faculty relationships are known to have a critical effect on whether black male students are marginalized or embraced in the college environment. The goal is to develop and use classroom teaching strategies that allow all students a place where they can safely express their personal experiences, examine differences among students from various backgrounds and social strata, and explore the particular issues relevant to their own cultural identity—in short, a nurturing place for all students in general and black men in particular.

Most college students seem to benefit from the attention of a mentor in a personal relationship, and African American male students seem to benefit as much as any other students, if not more so. Black students with mentors fare better during matriculation, complete college at higher rates, and express higher satisfaction with the college environment. A number of successful programs exist, any one of which may serve as a model for other campus administrators who are willing to commit to this proven means of enhancing the retention of African American male students.

Another factor besides mentoring that has been found to enhance the developmental growth of African American men in the college environment is the opportunity to serve in leadership roles among their peers. A variety of such opportunities for active participation are open to black students, from broad governance of large campuswide organizations to more intimate leadership in the relatively smaller membership of the typical black fraternity. Such variety provides black men with the chance to develop important interpersonal leadership skills, regardless of their areas of interest and their preferences for group affiliation: large or small, predominantly black or ethnically mixed, single-sex or coeducational.

Because of institutionalized stereotypes, African American male students are not often thought of as academically talented or gifted. However, when serious efforts to identify black men's actual abilities are made, students of the highest academic capability emerge. Yet even these brightest students encounter special difficulties as African American men, creating an important need for campus administrators to make serious efforts to retain these gifted students.

Unlike gifted black students, African American male student athletes are usually visible on most predominantly white campuses. Despite their visibility, these students have their own set of special needs that affect them as African Americans as well as students with special obligations and performance pressures. Because of their significant presence in athletic programs, especially football and basketball, any campuswide endeavor to enhance the retention of African American male students must include efforts to provide similar supports for the African American male athletes.

If there is one common theme in the lessons to be learned from the information presented in this book, it is that careful observation of the African American male students present on our college campuses today can provide a wealth of information about how to better serve these students and their brothers who will follow them. Because black men are often misunderstood thanks to our unwitting acquiescence to stereotypes and myths, the information they provide about black male culture and how to reinforce it and tap its positive energy is often overlooked. African American men are a fruitful resource on our campuses, part of the complex matrix of human experiences and interrelationships; we need to nurture and develop that resource for the enrichment of the entire campus community and all its members.

Further Reading

For further study of this subject, the following books are just a few of those that could be recommended by the authors in this volume:

Fleming, J. *Blacks in College: A Comparative Study of Students' Success in Black and in White Institutions.* San Francisco: Jossey-Bass, 1984.
Even after more than a decade, this is still one of the most comprehensive and revealing studies of African American students in recent time. The differences in the experiences of black men and black women on both white and black campuses offer insight into how student affairs administrators can assist in development of these students.

Helms, J. E. *Black and White Racial Identity: Theory, Research, and Practice.* Westport, Conn.: Greenwood, 1990.
A considerable number of research studies have demonstrated that an understanding of the racial and ethnic identity development of black students, particularly black male students, is critical to formulating programs to assist them in their adjustment to a predominantly white campus community and to aid in their personal development in that environment. This book offers a clear and comprehensive understanding of that racial identity development as it occurs in both black and white individuals.

Majors, R. and Billson, J. M. *Cool Pose: The Dilemma of Black Manhood in America.* San Francisco: New Lexington Press, 1992.
This book, although not focusing specifically on the college population, can provide the reader with important insight and appreciation of the more salient

aspects of black manhood in America today. It especially offers a positive perspective for some of the expressions of black maleness that are most misunderstood by the dominant culture.

Pascarella, E. T., and Terenzini, P. T. *How College Affects Students: Findings and Insights from Twenty Years of Research.* San Francisco: Jossey-Bass, 1991.
A considerable amount of research has already been conducted on the characteristics of African American male college students over the past several decades. This book, which reviews twenty years of research on the effects of the college environment on students, is an important resource to identify those studies that can offer insight into the issues confronting African American men on campus.

MICHAEL J. CUYJET is an associate professor in the Department of Educational and Counseling Psychology at the University of Louisville. A former student affairs practitioner for more than twenty years, he has served in both campus activities and general student affairs at several universities.

INDEX

Abercrombie, E., 46–47
Academic achievement: of African American men vs. women, 13–14; and Africentric identity, 24; at black vs. white colleges, 71–72; influences on, 31–33
African American male student athletes, 79–90, 94–95; advantages for, 82; college enrollment of, 79; demographics of, 80–81; graduation rates for, 79, 90; retention of, 83–89; stereotypes and expectations of, 81–82
African American men: enrolled in colleges, 1, 5–7, 43, 51, 70, 79; survey of college experiences of, 9–14. *See also* African American male student athletes; Gifted African American men
African American women: classroom discussion about, 38; enrolled in colleges, 5–6, 43, 79; faculty interaction with, 32; in Meyerhoff Program, 48; personal development of, 8–9; survey of college experiences of, 9–14
Africentric resistance model, 22, 22–24
Africentrism, 9, 94; and Africentric resistance model, 22–24; and involvement in Greek organizations, 28; and Nigrescence theory, 20–22
Albany (Georgia) State University, mentoring program, 47
Allen, W. R., 32, 71, 72
American Council on Education, 5, 70
Amey, M. J., 44
Anderson, J. L., 2, 8
Astin, A. W., 43, 45, 55, 82
Athletic facilities, 12

Baldwin, A. Y., 67
Bandura, A., 18, 20, 26–28
Banks, J. A., 68
Barol, B., 57, 61
Behar-Horenstein, L., 18
Belenky, M. F., 8
Bell Curve, The (Herrnstein and Murray), 68
Berg-Cross, L., 18, 19
Billson, J. M., 7, 9, 95–96
Bjork, L. G., 79
Black colleges, 32, 71–72
Black Male Initiative, 47

Black manhood issues, 38–39, 95–96
Black Man's Think Tank, 46–47
Black and White Racial Identity (Helms), 95
Blacks in College (Fleming), 71, 95
Bledsoe, T., 47
The Bridge, 48
Bryant, D. R., 18, 19

Career development: for African American male student athletes, 87–88, 89; theories of, 18
Carnegie Foundation for the Advancement of Teaching, 10
Carr, P., 83
Carter, D. J., 43
Center for the Study of Athletics, 80, 86
Challenging Athletes' Minds for Personal Success (CHAMPS), 84
Chambers, T., 56
Chapman, C. A., 48
Cheatham, H. E., 18, 19
Chester, 32
Chevez, E., 57
Chickering, A. W., 1, 18, 20, 82
Chiu, L. H., 68
Chordorow, N., 8
Christensen, P., 73
Chronicle of Higher Education Almanac, 1, 6, 14, 51
Clinchy, B. M., 8
Colangelo, N., 67, 69–70, 73
College Student Experiences Questionnaire (CSEQ), 1, 10–14, 15
Colleges: African American male student athletes' rate of graduation from, 79, 90; African Americans enrolled in, 1, 5–7, 43, 51, 70, 79; black vs. white, academic achievement at, 32, 71–72; parental graduation from, 14, 85; stereotypes of African American men in, 7–8, 81–82; white, negative perception of, 55
Collett, J. C., 46
Connolly, M. R., 10
Cool Pose (Majors and Billson), 95–96
Cooley, M. R., 68, 69
Cornell, D. G., 68, 69

ORDERING INFORMATION

NEW DIRECTIONS FOR STUDENT SERVICES is a series of paperback books that offers guidelines and programs for aiding students in their total development—emotional, social, and physical, as well as intellectual. Books in the series are published quarterly in Spring, Summer, Fall, and Winter and are available for purchase by subscription as well as individually.

SUBSCRIPTIONS cost $54.00 for individuals (a savings of 35 percent over single-copy prices) and $90.00 for institutions, agencies, and libraries. Standing orders are accepted. New York residents, add local sales tax for subscriptions. (For subscriptions outside the United States, add $7.00 for shipping via surface mail or $25.00 for air mail. Orders must be prepaid in U.S. dollars by check drawn on a U.S. bank or charged to VISA, MasterCard, or American Express.)

SINGLE COPIES cost $22.00 plus shipping (see below) when payment accompanies order. California, New Jersey, New York, and Washington, D.C., residents, please include appropriate sales tax. Canadian residents, add GST and any local taxes. Billed orders will be charged shipping and handling. No billed shipments to post office boxes. (Orders from outside the United States must be prepaid by check drawn on a U.S. bank or charged to VISA, MasterCard, or American Express.)

SHIPPING (SINGLE COPIES ONLY): $30.00 and under, add $5.50; to $50.00, add $6.50; to $75.00, add $7.50; to $100.00, add $9.00; to $150.00, add $10.00.

ALL PRICES are subject to change.

DISCOUNTS FOR QUANTITY ORDERS are available. Please write to the address below for information.

ALL ORDERS must include either the name of an individual or an official purchase order number. Please submit your order as follows:
   Subscriptions: specify series and year subscription is to begin
   Single copies: include individual title code (such as SS55)

MAIL ALL ORDERS TO:
   Jossey-Bass Publishers
   350 Sansome Street
   San Francisco, California 94104-1342

Phone subscription or single-copy orders toll-free at (888) 378-2537 or at (415) 433-1767 (toll call).Fax orders toll-free to: (800) 605-2665
FOR SUBSCRIPTION SALES OUTSIDE OF THE UNITED STATES, contact any international subscription agency or Jossey-Bass directly.

Statement of Ownership, Management, and Circulation

(Required by 39 USC 3685)

1. Publication Title	2. Publication Number										3. Filing Date
NEW DIRECTIONS FOR STUDENT SERVICES	0	1	6	4	–	7	9	7	0		9/18/97

4. Issue Frequency	5. Number of Issues Published Annually	6. Annual Subscription Price
QUARTERLY	4	$54 – indiv. $90 – instit.

7. Complete Mailing Address of Known Office of Publication *(Not printer) (Street, city, county, state, and ZIP+4)*

350 SANSOME STREET
SAN FRANCISCO, CA   94104
(SAN FRANCISCO COUNTY)

Contact Person
ROGER HUNT
Telephone
415 782 3232

8. Complete Mailing Address of Headquarters or General Business Office of Publisher *(Not printer)*

SAME AS ABOVE

9. Full Names and Complete Mailing Addresses of Publisher, Editor, and Managing Editor *(Do not leave blank)*

Publisher *(Name and complete mailing address)*
JOSSEY-BASS INC., PUBLISHERS
(ABOVE ADDRESS)

Editor *(Name and complete mailing address)*
JOHN SCHUH, PROFESSOR
PROFESSIONAL STUDIES IN EDUCATION
IOWA STATE UNIV/LAGOMARCINO HALL N247E
AMES, IA   50011

Managing Editor *(Name and complete mailing address)*
NONE

10. Owner *(Do not leave blank. If the publication is owned by a corporation, give the name and address of the corporation immediately followed by the names and addresses of all stockholders owning or holding 1 percent or more of the total amount of stock. If not owned by a corporation, give the names and addresses of the individual owners. If owned by a partnership or other unincorporated firm, give its name and address as well as those of each individual owner. If the publication is published by a nonprofit organization, give its name and address.)*

Full Name	Complete Mailing Address
SIMON & SCHUSTER	P.O. BOX 1172
	ENGLEWOOD CLIFFS, NJ 07632-1172

11. Known Bondholders, Mortgagees, and Other Security Holders Owning or Holding 1 Percent or More of Total Amount of Bonds, Mortgages, or Other Securities. If none, check box ▶ ☐ None

Full Name	Complete Mailing Address
SAME AS ABOVE	SAME AS ABOVE

12. Tax Status *(For completion by nonprofit organizations authorized to mail at special rates) (Check one)*
The purpose, function, and nonprofit status of this organization and the exempt status for federal income tax purposes:
☐ Has Not Changed During Preceding 12 Months
☐ Has Changed During Preceding 12 Months *(Publisher must submit explanation of change with this statement)*

PS Form **3526**, September 1995   *(See Instructions on Reverse)*

13. Publication Title	14. Issue Date for Circulation Data Below
NEW DIRECTIONS FOR STUDENT SERVICES	SUMMER 1997

15. Extent and Nature of Circulation		Average No. Copies Each Issue During Preceding 12 Months	Actual No. Copies of Single Issue Published Nearest to Filing Date
a. Total Number of Copies *(Net press run)*		1863	1942
b. Paid and/or Requested Circulation	(1) Sales Through Dealers and Carriers, Street Vendors, and Counter Sales *(Not mailed)*	234	56
	(2) Paid or Requested Mail Subscriptions *(Include advertiser's proof copies and exchange copies)*	892	894
c. Total Paid and/or Requested Circulation *(Sum of 15b(1) and 15b(2))* ▶		1126	950
d. Free Distribution by Mail *(Samples, complimentary, and other free)*		0	0
e. Free Distribution Outside the Mail *(Carriers or other means)*		118	145
f. Total Free Distribution *(Sum of 15d and 15e)* ▶		118	145
g. Total Distribution *(Sum of 15c and 15f)* ▶		1244	1095
h. Copies not Distributed	(1) Office Use, Leftovers, Spoiled	619	847
	(2) Returns from News Agents	0	0
i. Total *(Sum of 15g, 15h(1), and 15h(2))* ▶		1863	1942
Percent Paid and/or Requested Circulation *(15c / 15g x 100)*		91%	87%

16. Publication of Statement of Ownership
☒ Publication required. Will be printed in the ___WINTER 1997___ issue of this publication.
☐ Publication not required.

17. Signature and Title of Editor, Publisher, Business Manager, or Owner	Date
Susan E. Lewis SUSAN E. LEWIS DIRECTOR OF PERIODICALS	9/18/97

I certify that all information furnished on this form is true and complete. I understand that anyone who furnishes false or misleading information on this form or who omits material or information requested on the form may be subject to criminal sanctions (including fines and imprisonment) and/or civil sanctions (including multiple damages and civil penalties).

Instructions to Publishers

1. Complete and file one copy of this form with your postmaster annually on or before October 1. Keep a copy of the completed form for your records.

2. In cases where the stockholder or security holder is a trustee, include in items 10 and 11 the name of the person or corporation for whom the trustee is acting. Also include the names and addresses of individuals who are stockholders who own or hold 1 percent or more of the total amount of bonds, mortgages, or other securities of the publishing corporation. In item 11, if none, check the box. Use blank sheets if more space is required.

3. Be sure to furnish all circulation information called for in item 15. Free circulation must be shown in items 15d, e, and f.

4. If the publication had second-class authorization as a general or requester publication, this Statement of Ownership, Management, and Circulation must be published; it must be printed in any issue in October or, if the publication is not published during October, the first issue printed after October.

5. In item 16, indicate the date of the issue in which this Statement of Ownership will be published.

6. Item 17 must be signed.

Failure to file or publish a statement of ownership may lead to suspension of second-class authorization.

2357 049